DEWEY DECIMAL CLASSIFICATION
A Practice Manual of 23rd Edition

DEWEY DECIMAL CLASSIFICATION

A Practice Manual of 23rd Edition

By

DR. SANJAY K KAUSHIK

M. Lib. & Inf. Sc., Ph. D. (Lib. & Inf. Sc.)

PGDLAN (Hyderabad), APGDIT (Rohtak)

Assistant Librarian , M. D. University,

Rohtak-124 001 (HARYANA)

Ess Ess Publications

4837/24, Ansari Road, Darya Ganj,

New Delhi-110002

✆ : 23260807, 41563444

Fax : 011-41563334

E-mail: info@essessreference.com

url:http://www.essessreference.com

Dewey Decimal Classification
A Practical Manual for 23rd Edition

ISBN: 978-81-7000-672-5

Rs.750/-

First Published 2012

Published by:
Ess Ess Publications
4831/24, Ansari Road,
Darya Ganj,
New Delhi-110 002.
INDIA
Phones: 23260807, 41563444
Fax: 41563334
E-mail: info@essessreference.com
www.essessreference.com

Cover Design by *Patch Creative Unit*

Printed and bound in India at Salasar Imaging Systems.

Dedicated to

MY PARENTS

Smt. Meena Devi

and

Late Sh. J.N. Kaushik

Contents

Foreword

Classification is the basis of librarianship. Though there are several classification schemes, but Dewey Decimal Classification is undoubtedly the most used classification scheme. No other scheme in the world is as updated and revised as Dewey Decimal Classification. The new editions of DDC have been regularly brought out. The 23rd edition of DDC has been released in July 2011, which have incorporated many changes and added many new numbers.

The author of this excellent book provides a concise but comprehensive history of DDC. The changes in the form of additions, reallocations, etc have been provided in the book in a very informative manner. The methodology of explaining the process of classification with DDC is self-explanatory and by simply reading through this book, a library and information science student can easily learn "How to derive Class Numbers using DDC 23rd ?" The various features and provisions of DDC have been described in a planned and systematic way. The most difficult note i.e. **"Add note"** is explained in the book in a fabulous way with lot of suitable examples. A well-constructed self-check exercise is an essential component of any practice manual on classification and this book includes the component in a superb way.

The book has been written in a lucid language with suitable examples. Moreover, the book is comprehensive, up-to-date, and provides ample opportunity to learn classification practice.

I strongly believe that this book will help the classifiers who need to keep themselves updated to carry on work responsibilities. I am sure that the students and professionals will be greatly benefited from this book. The present book by Dr. Sanjay Kaushik is a commendable work.

Dr. (Mrs.) Ashu Shokeen
Professor
Dept. of Library & Information Science
Kurukshetra University Kurukshetra

Preface

Library is a growing organism. The collection of library grows continuously. As the size of the collection grows the need for arranging the documents systematically according to a classification scheme arises. It is almost impossible for a big library to survive without a library classification scheme. Hence library classification is taught as a compulsory subject in the various courses of library and information science all over the World. A system of library classification that flashed across the inquiring mind of young Melvil Louis Kossuth Dewey (known as Melvil Dewey) in 1873 is still the most popular classification scheme. The modern library classification begins with Dewey Decimal Classification (DDC). DDC was devised by Melvil Dewey in 1876. Now the scheme has an incredible history of 136 years of boundless success. This scheme is widely being used in majority of the libraries in about 150 countries. Despite the ever-mounting criticism of its faulty approach and the 19th century structure, its popularity has always shown a spiking graph. No doubt, for a classification system to maintain its relevancy, it must be continually revised and expanded. The DDC has a continuous revision policy. The Decimal Classification Editorial Policy Committee (EPC) is responsible for revisions and expansions in DDC. It is the result of continuous revisions that the 23rd edition of DDC has been published in July 2011. No other classification scheme has published so many editions. Some welcome changes have been made in DDC 23.

The present book is an attempt to explain with suitable examples the salient provisions of DDC 23. The book is written in a simple and lucid language so that even the students may not face any difficulty. The examples in the book are explained in a step-by-step procedure. The first two chapters are devoted to introduction and major changes in DDC 23. Chapter 3 is devoted to the schedules. In the chapters 4 to 9 Tables 1 to 6 have been dealt with. Chapter 10 deals with the treatment of groups of persons. Self-check exercise for the practice of the students follows this chapter. The three summaries are appended at the end of the book for ready reference of the users.

It is hoped that this book is of great help and usefulness to the library professionals at large, library classifiers in general and Library and Information Science students in particular.

Though the utmost care has been taken, errors or omissions might persist. Constructive criticism and suggestions for improvement from the intelligent readers are welcome.

I first and foremost wish to convey my debt of gratitude to Dr. (Mrs.) Ashu Shokeen, Professor of Library and Information Science, Kurukshetra University, Kurukshetra, whose constant motivation and blessings made me capable of taking such assignment as a challenge. My association with her since my days at Kurukshetra University, Kurukshetra as a student has made me a firm believer in 'no *looking behind until the work is complete'*. My heartfelt huge thanks are also due to Prof. Prem Singh,

University Librarian, M D University, Rohtak under whose able and dynamic leadership, I learnt new dimensions of practical library classification. My special thanks are also due to my colleagues, friends and well-wishers whose constant encouragement has been a great source of strength in my academic endeavor. I must also put on record my appreciation to Mr. Sumit Sethi of Ess Ess Publications for expeditious publication of this book.

Finally, I want as always to express my appreciation, gratitude and thanks towards my family. The lessons of hard work, sincerity, truthfulness and foresightedness taught by my mother are the perennial source of inspiration and strength for me. My wife Mrs. Nishi is a superb house maker and that gives me ample time to devote towards my academic activities. While I spend my quality time with my daughter Anshu and son Adhav, it makes me relaxed and refreshed which works as a booster to my energy.

Dr. Sanjay K Kaushik

1

Introduction to DDC 23

HISTORICAL BACKGROUND

Melvil Dewey: A Brief Sketch

The deviser of DDC was an American Librarian named Melvil Dewey, whose full name is Melvil Louis Kossuth Dewey. He was born on 10th September 1851 in the Adms Centre city of New York State. Melvil was a son of small businessman and at the age of five he said I will arrange my mother's larder. In 1870 he took admission in Amherst College for his higher studies and at the age of 23 he got the Bachelor degree in 1874. During his studies in the college he joined the college library as a student assistant and after getting the graduation he was appointed as Assistant Librarian of this college[1]. As student assistant, he prepared a scheme for classifying the books of Amherst College during 1873-75 and got his classification scheme published in the year 1876.

Later Melvil was appointed as Librarian of New York State Library. In 1887 Melvil established the first library science school in Columbia University and started teaching. Melvil also has the distinction of being editor and publisher of the first magazine of library science named "Library Journal". Apart from this he also played a vital role in the establishment and directing of several institutions like: American Library Association, Spelling Reform Association, Metric Bureau, British Library Association, Readers and Writers company, Library Bureau, etc[2].

On 30th December 1931 the profession of Librarianship had lost this great librarian but the profession will remain indebted forever to this great personality.

ORIGIN AND GROWTH OF DDC

Melvil Dewey visited a number of libraries before devising his classification scheme. He sought suggestions in this regard from W T Harris, Jacob Schwart and Natale Battezzati. He applied the scheme for experiment to Amherst College Library during 1873- 76 and after its success he published his scheme in 1876. The title of this scheme was "A Classification and subject index for cataloguing and arranging the books and pamphlets of a library". This edition received a warm welcome from American Librarians. The size of first edition was very small. It contained only 44 pages out of which 14 pages were devoted to introduction, 18 pages were devoted to index and only 12 pages were devoted to schedules.

The second edition under the name of Melvil Dewey was brought out in 1885. This edition unlike the first edition had the name of Melvil Dewey as author. The title was changed as "Decimal classification and relative index for arranging, cataloguing and indexing public and private libraries and for pamphlets, clippings, notes scrapbooks, index, resumes, etc." After the death of Melvil Dewey, in 1951 his name was added to the title and in 15th revised edition title was again changed as "Dewey Decimal

Classification and relative index". This title is still unchanged upto the 23rd edition published in July 2011.

A brief account of all the editions of DDC is given in the following table[3].

Edition number	Year of publication	Number of volumes	Total pages
First	1876	One	44
Second	1885	One	314
Third	1888	One	416
Fourth	1891	One	466
Fifth	1894	One	467
Six	1899	One	511
Seven	1911	One	792
Eight	1913	One	850
Ninth	1915	One	856
Tenth	1919	One	940
Eleventh	1922	One	988
Twelfth	1927	One	1243
Thirteenth	1932	One	1647
Fourteenth	1942	One	1927
Fifteenth	1951	One	1716
Fifteenth (revised)	1952	One	1927
Sixteenth	1958	Two	2439
Seventeenth	1965	Two	2480
Eighteenth	1971	Three	2692
Nineteenth	1979	Three	4779
Twentieth	1989	Four	3273
Twenty first	1996	Four	4037
Twenty second	2003	Four	3983
Twenty third	2011	Four	4276

Since the publication of its first edition in 1876, the Dewey Decimal Classification (DDC) system has crossed many milestones. Some major milestones are mentioned in the below table[4]:-

Year	Milestones
1876	The first edition entitled "A Classification and Subject Index for Cataloguing and Arranging Books and Pamphlets of a library" is published
1885	The second edition is published under the name of great Melvil Dewey
1900	The first abridged edition of the DDC is published
1916	The Decimal Classification Advisory Committee- the American Library Association's first advisory committee- is appointed
1923	The DDC editorial office moves to the Library of Congress in Washington, DC
1930	The Library of Congress begins to print Dewey numbers on catalog cards
1931	The great Melvil Dewey dies
1937	The Decimal Classification Committee is established
1953	The Decimal Classification Editorial Committee is reconstituted to represent the American Library Association (ALA), Forest Press and the Library of Congress to guide to editorial development of the DDC.
1958	The 16th edition of the DDC is published. This edition was edited under agreement between the LC and Forest Press.
1988	Forest Press becomes a division of OCLC
1993	OCLC Forest Press publishes Electronic Dewey, the first library classification scheme in electronic form
1996	The 21st edition of the DDC for Windows are published, making it the first time print and electronic formats are published simultaneously
2000	WebDewey in CORC is published
2002	WebDewey and abridged WebDewey are published
2003	22nd edition of DDC is published
2008	First time EPC chairperson was elected from outside North America
2011	23rd edition of DDC is published

Classifying with the DDC

Classifying a work with DDC requires determining the subject, the disciplinary focus, and if applicable the approach or form.

DETERMINING THE SUBJECT OF A WORK

Classifying a work properly depends first upon determining the subject of the work in hand. A key element in determining the subject is the author's intent. Some tips for determining the subject of a work are as follows.

1. The title is often a clue to the subject, but should never be the sole source of analysis. For example, "Who Moved My Cheese?" is a work on coping with change, not a work related to the culinary arts. Likewise, a title with specific terms that are subdivisions of a field may in fact use such terms symbolically to represent the broader topic. For example, titles containing terms like chromosomes, DNA, double helix, genes, and genomes may use these terms symbolically to represent the whole subject of biochemical genetics.
2. The table of contents may list the main topics discussed. Chapter headings may substitute for the absence of a table of contents. Chapter subheadings often prove useful.
3. The preface or introduction usually states the author's purpose. If a foreword is provided, it often indicates the subject of the work and suggests the place of the work in the development of thought on the subject. The book jacket or accompanying material may include a summary of the subject content.
4. A scan of the text itself may provide further guidance or confirm preliminary subject analysis.
5. Bibliographical references and index entries are

sources of subject information.

6. Cataloguing copy from centralized cataloguing services is often helpful by providing subject headings, classification numbers, and notes. Such copy appears in online services, and on the verso of the title page of many U S, Australian, British, and Canadian books as part of Cataloguing-in-publication (CIP) data. Data from these sources should be verified with the book in hand, since the cataloguing record is based on prepublication information.
7. Occasionally, consultation of outside sources such as reviews, reference works, and subject experts may be required to determine the subject of the work.

DETERMINING THE DISCIPLINE OF A WORK

After determining the subject, the classifier must then select the proper discipline, or field of study, of the work.

The guiding principle of the DDC is that a work is classed in the discipline for which it is intended, rather than the discipline from which the work derives. This enables works that are used together to be found together. For example, a general work by a zoologist on agricultural pest control should be classed in agriculture, not zoology, along with other works on agricultural pest control.

Once the subject has been determined, and information on the discipline has been found, the classifier will turn to the schedules. The summaries are a good means of mental navigation. The headings and notes in the schedules themselves and the Manual provide much guidance. The relative index may help by suggesting the disciplines in which a subject is normally treated.

If the relative index is used, the classifier must still rely on the structure of the classification and various aids throughout to arrive at the proper place to classify a work. Even the most promising Relative Index citations must be verified in the schedules; the schedules are the only place where all the information about coverage and use of the numbers may be found.

MORE THAN ONE SUBJECT IN THE SAME DISCIPLINE

A work may include multiple subjects treated separately or in relation to one another from the viewpoint of a single discipline. Use the following guidelines in determining the best placement for the work:

1. Class a work dealing with interrelated subjects with the subject that is being acted upon. This is called the rule of application, and work takes precedence over any other rule. For instance, class an analytical work dealing with Shakespeare's influence on Keats with Keats. Similarly, class a work on the influence of the great Depression on the 20th century American art with American art.
2. Class a work on two subjects with the subject receiving fuller treatment.
3. If two subject receive equal treatment, and are not used to introduce or explain one another, class the work with the subject whose number comes first in the DDC schedules. This is called the first-of-two rule. For example, a history dealing equally with the United States and Japan, in which the United States is discussed first and is given first in the title, is classed with the history of Japan because 952 Japan precedes 973 United States.

   Sometimes, specific instructions are given to use numbers that do not come first in the schedules. For example, at 598, the note "class comprehensive works on warm-blooded vertebrates in 599" tells the classifier to ignore the first-of-two rule and class a work on birds (598) and mammals (599) in 599, which is the comprehensive number for warm-blooded vertebrates.

Also disregard the first-of-two rule when the two topics are the two major subdivisions of a subject. For example, collection systems (628.142) and distribution systems (628.144) taken together constitute 628.14 Collection and distribution systems. Works covering both of these topics are classed in 628.14 (not 628.142).

4. Class a work on three or more subjects that are all subdivisions of a broader subject in the first higher number that includes them all. This is called the rule of three. For example, a history of China (951), Japan (952) and India (954) is classed with the history of Asia (950).

5. Subdivisions beginning with zero should be avoided if there is a choice between 0 and 1-9 at the same point in the hierarchy of the notation. Similarly, subdivisions beginning with 00 should be avoided when there is a choice between 00 and 0. This is called the rule of zero. For ecxample, a biography of an American Methodist missionary in China belongs in 266 Missions. The content of the work can be expressed in three different numbers:

266.0092	biography of a missionary
266.02373051	foreign missions of the US in China
266.76092	biography of a United Methodist Church missionary

The last number is used since it has no zero at the fourth position.

MORE THAN ONE DISCIPLINE

Treating a subject from the point of view of more than one discipline is different from treating several subjects in one discipline. Use the following guidelines in determining the best placement for the work:

1. Use the interdisciplinary number provided in the schedules or relative Index if one is given. An important consideration in using such an interdisciplinary number is that the work must contain significant material on the discipline in which the interdisciplinary number is found. For example, 305.231 is provided for interdisciplinary works on child development. However, if a work that is interdisciplinary with respect to child development gives little emphasis to social development and a great deal of emphasis to the psychological and physical development of the child (155.4 and 612.65, respectively), class it in 155.4 (the first number in the schedules of the next two obvious choices). In short, interdisciplinary numbers are not absolute; they are to be used only when applicable.
2. Class works not given an interdisciplinary number in the discipline given the fullest treatment in the work. For example, a work dealing with both the scientific and the engineering principles of electrodynamics is classed 537.6 if the engineering aspects are introduced primarily for illustrative purposes, but in 621.31 if the basic scientific theories are only preliminary to the author's exposition of engineering principles and practices.
3. When classifying interdisciplinary works, do not overlook the possibilities of main class 000 Computer science, information & general works, e.g. 080 for a collection of interviews of famous people from various disciplines.

Any other situation is treated in the same fashion as those found in the instructions at More Than One Subject in the Same Discipline.

TABLE OF LAST RESORT

When several numbers have been found for the work in hand, and each seems as good as next, the following table of last resort (in order of preference) may be used as a guideline in the absence of any other rule:

Table of last resort

1. Kinds of things
2. Parts of things
3. Materials from which things, kinds, or parts are made
4. Properties of things, kinds, parts, or materials
5. Processes within things, kinds, parts, or materials
6. Operations upon things, kinds, parts, or materials
7. Instrumentalities for performing such operations

For example, surveillance by border patrols could be classed in either 363.285 Border patrols, or 363.232 Patrols and surveillance. Choose 363.285 since border patrols are a kind of police services, while patrols and surveillance are processes performed by police services.

Note: *Don't apply this table or any other guideline if it appears to disregard the author's intention and emphasis.*

NOTES IN DDC 23

To guide the classifier at the point where need is felt, a vertiginous variety of notes are provided in DDC. Notes are important because they supply information that is not obvious in the notational hierarchy or in the heading with regard to order, structure, subordination, and other matters. Notes may appear in the record for a number or a span of numbers. Notes may also appear at the beginning of a table. Footnotes are used for instructions that apply to multiple subdivisions of a class, or to a topic within a class. Broadly these notes are categorized in four categories, which are explained in the following paragraphs:

1. Notes that describe what is found in a class: This category of notes consists of various notes, which tell the classifier to what is to be classified under this class. *Definition notes* indicate the meaning of a term in the heading. For example:

364 Criminology

Crime and its alleviation

This note defines that the documents dealing with crime and its alleviation should be classified under the number 364.

Scope notes indicate whether the meaning of the number is narrower or broader than is apparent from the heading. For example:

005.3 Programs

Software, firmware, middleware

Number-built notes identify and explain the source of built numbers included in the schedules and tables. Built numbers are occasionally included in the schedules or tables to provide additional information or to indicate exceptions to regular add instructions. For example:

353.132 63 Foreign service

Number built according to instructions under 352-354

Class here consular and diplomatic services

Former-heading notes are provided only when the heading associated with a class number in the previous edition has been altered to such a degree that the new heading bears little or no resemblance to the previous heading, even though the meaning of the number has remained substantially the same. For example:

659.131 5 Industrial advertising

Former heading: Advertising directed to vocational uses

Variant-name notes are given for synonyms or near synonyms. For example:

005.746 Data compression

Variant names: data compaction, file compression

Class-here notes list major topics in a class. These topics may be broader or narrower than the heading, overlap it, or define another way of looking at essentially the same material. Topics in class-here notes are considered to approximate the whole of the class. For example:

025.4 Subject analysis and control

Class here standards for subject analysis and control

2. Notes that identify topics in standing room: This type of notes is called including notes. Including notes identify topics that have "standing room" in the number where the note is found. Standing room numbers provide a location for topics with relatively few works written about them, but whose literature may grow in the future, at which time they may be assigned their own number. For example:

005.52 Word processing

Including grammar checkers, spelling checkers, style checkers

3. Notes that describe what is found in other classes: This type of notes lead the classifier to interrelated topics, or distinguish among numbers in the same notational hierarchy. In DDC 23 these notes are provided as class-elsewhere notes, and see and see also notes. *Class elsewhere notes* are used to show preference order, to lead to the comprehensive or inter-disciplinary number, to override the first-of-two rule, or to lead to broader or narrower topics in the same hierarchical array that might otherwise be overlooked. An example of class elsewhere notes is as under:

616.891 8 Drug therapy

Class drug stock therapy in 616.891 2

See references lead from a stated or implied comprehensive number for a concept to the component parts of that concept in a different notational hierarchy. A see reference may point to a specific number, or to a concept scattered throughout the schedules. Each see reference begins with the word "For" and appears in italics. For example:

666.3 Pottery

Class here comprehensive works on clay technology

Class pottery in the narrow sense of earthenware in 666.6

For techniques and procedures, see 666.44; for specific types of pottery, see 666.5-666.6; for structural clay products, see 666.73

See-also references lead the classifier to related topics. They are reminders that minor differences in wording and context can imply differences in classification. Each see-also reference appears in italics. For example:

641.87 Preparing beverages

Class interdisciplinary works on beverages in 641.2

See also 641.62 for cooking with beverages

4. Notes that explain changes or irregularities in the schedules and tables: This category also include various notes which bring to the notice of the classifier the changes or irregularities in the schedules as well as tables. Discontinued notes indicate that all or part of the contents of a number have been moved to a more general number in the same hierarchy, or have been dropped entirely. For example:

[653.424 2-.424 5] Isaac Pitman, Benn Pitman, Graham, Munson systems
Numbers discontinued; class in 653.424

Relocation notes state that all or part of the contents of number have been moved to a different number. For example:

[537.67] Quantum electrodynamics
Relocated to 530.143 3

Do-not-use notes instruct the classifier not to use all or part of the regular standard subdivision notation or an add table provision, but instead to use a special provision or standard subdivision notation at a broader number. When the whole standard subdivision is removed from use, the note appears under a bracketed standard subdivision; when only part of the standard subdivision is displaced, the part displaced is specified. For example:

[026.000 68] Management
Do not use; class in 025.19

028.108 Reviews with respect to kinds of persons
Do not use for reviews of works for specific kinds of users; class in 028.16

NOTATION USED IN DDC

In DDC Arabic numerals have been used to represent each class. The first digit in each three-digit number represents the main class. For example, 300 represents social science. The second digit in each three-digit number indicates the division. For example, 300 is used for general works on the social sciences, 320 for Political science, 330 for Economics. The third digit in each three-digit number indicates the section. Thus, 330 is used for general works on Economics. 331 for Labour economics, 332 for Financial economics, 333 for Economics of land & energy. The DDC uses the convention that no number should have fewer than three digits; zeros are used to fill out numbers.

A decimal point or dot is inserted between the third and fourth digit in a class number. This dot is not a decimal point in the mathematical sense, but a psychological pause to break the monotony of numerical digits and to ease the transcription and copying the class number. A number should never end in a zero anywhere to the right of the decimal point.

STRUCTURE OF DDC

DDC is a hierarchical scheme of classification, which proceeds from the general to the specific. The basic arrangement is by discipline, and a specific subject can occur in any number of disciplines. The universe of subject is divided into ten main classes, which are enumerated in First Summary. Each main class is further divided into ten divisions. These hundred divisions are enumerated in Second Summary. Further each division is divided into ten sections. These thousand sections are enumerated in Third Summary. The hierarchical structure of DDC can be understood by following example:

300	Social science
330	Economics
332	Financial economics
332.1	Banks

OUTLINE OF DDC 23

The DDC 23 is composed of following major parts in four volumes:

Volume 1

1. New features in edition 23: A brief explanation of the special features and changes in DDC 23

2. Introduction: A description of the DDC and how to use it

3. Glossary: Short definitions of terms used in the DDC

4. Index to the Introduction and glossary

5. Manual : A guide to the use of the DDC that is made up primarily of extended discussions of problem area in the application of DDC. Information in the manual is arranged by numbers in the tables and schedules.

6. Tables : Six numbered tables of notation that can be added to class numbers to provide greater specificity

7. Lists that compare Editions 22 and 23 : Relocations and Discontinuations; Reused Numbers

Volume 2

1. DDC Summaries : The top three levels of the DDC

2. Schedules: The organization of knowledge from 000-599

Volume 3

1. Schedules: The organization of knowledge from 600-999

Volume 4

1. Relative Index: An alphabetical list of subjects with the disciplines in which they are treated sub-arranged alphabetically under each entry

SUMMARIES

In volume 2 of DDC 23, three summaries have been provided at pages v to xvi. The First Summary contains The Ten Main Classes. The Second Summary contains The Hundred Divisions and The Thousand Sections are contained in the Third Summary. The students are advised to go time and again through these summaries so that they can become familiar with these summaries. All these summaries are provided at the end of this book.

HOW TO MOVE IN THE SECHDULES

The arrangement of schedules in DDC is according to class numbers starting from 000 to 599 in volume 2 and 600 to 999 in volume 3. Just hold on the volume in right hand and drop the pages, keep your eye on the top of the page you can notice the class number on the both sides of the page. The procedure is the same as of consulting a dictionary but the only difference is that dictionary is arranged according to alphabets and DDC according to numerals.

HOW TO BUILD A CLASS NUMBER

The number building process of DDC is a step-by-step process. The simplest way building a class number according to DDC is as under:

Step 1 : Select the one of the ten main classes in First Summary, which suits most to your title. In case you have no idea about the title's main class then consult the index (for more details see How to Consult the index? the next heading.)

Step 2 : Search among the ten divisions of that main class in Second Summary and select the most suitable one.

Step 3 : Search the ten sections of that division in the Third Summary and select the most suitable one.

Step 4 : Go to the schedule of that section and search

the appropriate number.

Step 5 : Write down the base number and, if required, follow the instructions and/ or add standard subdivisions.

Step 6 : Insert a dot between the third and fourth digit.

Let us demonstrate this procedure with the help of an example:

Title	**Encyclopaedia of Hindu Pilgrimages**
Step 1	It is clear from the title that the document belongs to the Hindu pilgrimages. Hinduism is a religion. One of the ten main classes is Religion i.e. 200. Hence we have selected 200.
Step 2	Go to Second Summary under 200 200 and 210 are devoted to general treatment of religions and 220 to 280 are devoted to Christianity. Hence the only number left is 290 which will cover all the religions other than Christianity.
Step 3	Go to Third Summary under 290, there is a section 294 Religions of Indic origin. Hinduism is of Indic origin. Hence select this number.
Step 4	Go to schedule and consult the notations under 294. Here you will find 294.5 Hinduism.
Step 5	Write down the base number i.e. 294.5. (Please note sometimes the base number given in the add note is different from the number you have written. In this case the base number given in add note is to be written). Go further and you will find an instruction at 294.51-.53. By following this instruction you will go to the schedule under number 201 to 203 and search a number for pilgrimages. Under 203 you will find a number 203.51 Pilgrimages. This number you will write in the rough work portion. From this number now you have to omit the number which have been given between the words "following and in" in the add note. Now you will suffix (add at the last of the number) the remaining number to the base number already written. Now you have added number for Hindu and Pilgrimages and your title is encyclopaedia of Hindu Pilgrimages. Go to Table 1 and select a number for Encyclopaedia in

Standard Subdivisions. The right choice is -03. (See details in Chapter 4). Add this number at the last of the number built so far.

Step 6 The number is complete and Insert a dot between the third and fourth digit. As a matter of convenience give a blank space after every three digits starting from the sixth digit.

The above example will look like this according to the pattern followed in this book:

Encyclopaedia of Hindu Pilgrimages	**294.535 103**
Base Number	294.5
Instruction	Add to base number 294.5 the numbers following 20 in 201 -203
Pilgrimages	203.51
Encyclopaedia (Table 1)	-03 (s.s.)
	=294.5+351+03
Class No.	294.535 103

HOW TO CONSULT THE RELATIVE INDEX

The relative index is so named because it relates subjects to disciplines. In the schedules, subjects are distributed among disciplines; in the relative index, subjects are arranged alphabetically, with terms identifying the disciplines in which they are treated subarranged alphabetically under them[5]. For example:

Marriage	306.81
arts	700.454 3
	T3C-354 3
customs	392.5
ethics	173
religion	205.63
Buddhism	294.356 3

Christianity	241.63
Hinduism	294.548 63
Islam	297.563
Judaism	296.363
folklore	398.27
history and criticism	398.354
law	346.016
literature	808.803 543
history and criticism	809.933 543
specific literatures	T3B-080 354 3
history and criticism	T3B-093 543
music	781.587
personal religion	204.41
Buddhism	294.344 41
Christianity	248.4
Hinduism	294.544 1
Islam	297.577
Judaism	296.74
religion	204.41
Christianity	248.4
Islam	297.577
Judaism	296.74
religious doctrine	202.2
Christianity	234.165
religious law	208.4
Christianity	265.5
Judaism	296.444
liturgy	296.454 4

see *also* Public worship

social theology 201.7

Christianity 261.83581

In the above example, marriage as a subject is subarranged under various disciplines and the classifier has to opt for a discipline most suitable to the document in hand. The relative index is primarily an index to the DDC as a system. It includes most terms found in the schedules and tables, and terms with literary warrant for concepts represented by schedules and tables. The relative index is not exhaustive. If the term sought is not found, the classifier should try a broader term, or consult the schedules and tables directly. The classifier should always consult the schedules and tables before he/she applies a number found in relative index.

REFERENCES

1. Sharma (Pandey S K). Practical approach to DDC: Dewey Decimal Classification made simple. 1998. New Delhi; Ess Ess Publications. pp3-4.
2. Gautam (J N) and Niranjan Singh. Dewey Decimal Classification: Practical analysis (Ed. 19 & 20). 1996. Agra; Y K Publishers. pp. 1-2.
3. M. D. University, Rohtak. Library Classification: Practice. Lesson for Bachelor of Library & Information Science students. 2003. New Delhi; Excel Books. p.8.
4. http:/www.oclc.org
5. Dewey, Melvil. Dewey Decimal classification and relative index. Edition 23. Dublin, OCLC, 2011.

2

Major Changes in DDC 23

Classification is the basis of librarianship. In each library one or another scheme of classification is used. For a classification system to maintain its relevancy, it must be continually revised and expanded. The Decimal Classification Editorial Policy Committee (EPC) is responsible for revisions and expansions in DDC. The 23rd edition of DDC has been published in July 2011. A number of welcome changes have been incorporated in this edition.

MAJOR CHANGES IN DDC 23

Edition 23 is a complete overhaul of the representation of groups of people, significant revisions of several standard subdivisions, numerous updates throughout the tables and schedules. It also includes some structural changes. These changes can be discussed under two subheadings as under[1].

CHANGES IN TABLES

The phrase "kinds of persons" is replaced with "groups of people". The caption "History and description with respect to" is entirely deleted from table 1 at -08 and elsewhere in DDC. The caption "Social groups" at 305 is substituted with "Groups of people". The caption "Persons treatment" in table 1 at 092 is changed with "Biography". There is slight change at -09 in table 1 too, "Historical, geographic, persons treatment is now "History, geographic treatment, biography". There is also a significant expansion for collected biography of groups of people by various attributes in table 1 under -092.

Some selected changes are provided below:

Table 1. Standard Subdivisions

0141	Discourse analysis (This is new number introduced in DDC23)
-0286	Green technology (Environmental technology) *(This caption is changed from waste technology)*
-0721	Research methods *(This is new number introduced in DDC23)*
-081	People by gender or sex *(This caption is revised and expanded)*
-0865	People by marital status *(This caption is changed from marriage status)*
-0867	Transgender and intersex people *(This is new number introduced in DDC23)*
-09	History, geographic treatment, biography *(This caption is changed from* Historical, geographic, persons treatment*)*
-0925	Collected biography of people by specific gender or sex; age groups; relationships *(This is new number introduced in DDC23)*
-0928	Collected biography of members of specific religious group *(This is new number introduced in DDC23)*

Table 2. Geographic Areas, Historical Periods, Persons

-31	China to 420
-32	Egypt to 640
-34	South Asia to 647
	(Note: under these captions, time is added for the first time and below to many of these ancient world numbers an add note is added instructing to add the numbers from the modern world)
-46911	Viana do Castelo district [formerly -46912]
-46912	Barga district
	(This is new number introduced in DDC23)
-4861	Skane County
-4862	Blekinge County
-4863	Kalmar County
	(-486 is expanded and new nos. from -4861 to -4869 are introduced in DDC 23)

Table 3B. Subdivisions for Works by or about more Than one Author

–3082	Autobiographical and biographical fiction *(This is new number introduced in DDC23)*
-308768	Alternative histories
	(This is new number introduced in DDC23)

Table 3C. Notation to be added where instructed in table 3B, 700.4, 791.4, 808 809

–32	Travel and geography
	(This caption is changed from Places)

Table 4. Subdivisions of individual languages and language families

-01430285	Computer Applications
-0145	Pragmatics
-0147	Languages for special purposes
-0188	Corpus linguistics
-823	Punctuation
	(These are the new numbers and two of these are further expanded too)

Table 5. Ethnic and national groups

-591	Romanians
-5992	Friulians
-5994	Ladins
-5996	Romansch
-5998	Sardinians and Corsicans
-91454	Bihari
-9517	Hakka

Note: *All these numbers are new introduced in DDC 23. In addition to these many other numbers like -935, -954, -959, -9838, -9922 are expanded in DDC 23)*

Table 6. Languages

-599 is expanded and many other new numbers are added:

-5992	Friulian language
-5994	Ladin language
-5996	Romansch language
-5998	Sardinian and Corsican
-699	Galician
-91489	Divehi (Maldivian)
-95978	Yao
-99482	Tongan (Tonga)
-99484	Niue (Niuean)
-9959	Eastern Fijian languages

CHANGES IN SCHEDULES

A number of new numbers, relocations, revisions and expansions have been provided in DDC 23. These are being discussed class wise:-

Computer science, information & general works:

The schedules 004-006 Data processing Computer science has been completely updated. Many new numbers like 003.72 Networks, 004.167 Hand-held computing devices, 004.568 Semiconductor devices, 004.6782 Cloud computing, 004.695 Internet telephony, and subdivisions, etc. have been included in the schedules. Certain relocations have also been made such as class number for Embedded computer systems is relocated to 006.22 from 004.1. World Wide Web is relocated in 025.042 (Library Science) from 004.678 (Computer Science). Data mining is relocated to 006.312 from 005.74. Overseas information libraries relocated to 027.5 from 027.65.

The class number for general encyclopedic works in Serbian and Croatian (037.82 in DDC 22) is bifurcated in 037.82 for Serbian and 037.83 for Croatian. The class number [001.432] is discontinued in DDC 23 and the class number for Historical methods already available at 907.2 is to be used. The class numbers for Alphabetic catalog of nonprivate libraries; private and family libraries; subject auction catalogs; subject sales catalogs [017.5-017.8] are discontinued and relocated in 017.1-017.4. The numbers [018] Catalogs arranged by author, main entry, date, or register number and [019] Dictionary catalogs are also discontinued and relocated to 017. The numbers for pre-coordinate indexing [025.482] and coordinate and post-coordinate indexing [025.484] are also discontinued and relocated to 025.47.

Philosophy and Psychology

Two new numbers 150.1985 for Personal construct psychology and 150.1988 for Positive Psychology are introduced in the psychology main class. The schedule 155 of Differential and developmental psychology is revised and expanded. Now under 155 a table is provided with add notes, so that the different aspects of individual psychology can be applied to the numbers identified with *. In Philosophical logic 160, under standard subdivision .1 Philosophy and theory, provision of specific systems of classical and non-classical logic and its subdivisions is made as 160.119 and 160.1198. Certain new numbers like:

176.2 Ethics of reproductive technology; 176.22 Ethics of Human cloning; 176.3 Ethics of Birth control; and 176.4 Ethics of Sexual relations are added.

The class number for inter-personal relationship is relocated to 155.4192 from 155.418. The relocations made in psychology schedule include: from 155.6 (Psychology of adults), Sensory perception, movement, emotions, physiological drives of adults is relocated to 152, conscious mental processes and intelligence to 153 and applied psychology of adults to 158. The relocations are also made in the schedule of Philosophy. Some of these are: From 197 Philosophy of former Soviet Union; Philosophy of Azerbaijan relocated to 199.4754, Philosophy of Armenia relocated to 199.4756, Philosophy of Georgia relocated to 199.4758, Philosophy of Moldova relocated to 199.476, Philosophy of Ukraine relocated to 199.477, Philosophy of Belarus relocated to 199.478, Philosophy of Lithuania relocated to 199.478, Philosophy of Latvia relocated to 199.4796, and Philosophy of Estonia relocated to 199.4798.

A few class numbers are discontinued and relocated. These are: [155.334] Bisexuality relocated to 155.343; [155.60866] Adults in general by sexual orientation relocated to 155.34; [155.6089] Ethnic and national groups relocated to 155.82; and [155.63] Adults by gender or sex relocated to 155.33.

Religion

In main class for religion the numbers for codex iruis canonici (262.94) and Eastern churches (281.5) are expanded and many new numbers like 262.941 General norms, 262.942 The people of God, .943 Teaching mission of the church, 281.52 Eastern Catholic churches, .54 Saint Thomas Christian churches, etc are introduced. 296.76 for Persons experiencing illness, trouble, bereavement is also a new number in DDC 23.

The class numbers for creeds of Eastern Catholic churches relocated to 238.15, creeds of Saint Thomas Christian churches relocated to 238.154, creeds of Oriental Orthodox churches relocated to 238.16, creeds of Assyrian Church of the East relocated to 238.18, from 238.19. Hadith (Traditions) [297.124] is discontinued and relocated to 297.125. The class numbers [297.09023] and [.09024] for 14th and 15th century are discontinued and relocated to higher order i.e. 297.09022.

Social sciences

In the schedule of social sciences numerous new numbers are introduced. These are: 302.343 Bullying, 332.04246 Emigrant remittances, 335.4346 Asian national variants, 340.114 Justice, 341.2421 Council of Europe, 347.057 Legal costs and fees, 361.43 Self-help groups, 362.682 Elder abuse, 363.3494 Tsunamis, 371.391 Waldorf method, 378.1035 Industry relations, 391.72 Finger rings, and 393.93 Funerals.

The class number 320.54 Nationalism is revised and termed as Nationalism, regionalism, internationalism. Under 320.54 the provision of adding area table is made. The class number 304.2082 for factors affecting social behavior of women is relocated from 305.42. Ideologies based on groups of people have been relocated to 320.56 from 320.508. The number for Appellate procedure in criminal courts is relocated to 345.144 from 347.08. Young people as parents relocated to 362.7874 from 362.7085. The class number for explosives is relocated to 363.1798 from 363.33. The class number for riddles as jokes by known authors is relocated from 398.6 to 808.882.

A large number of class numbers in social science schedule are discontinued and relocated. Such as: Women by social and economic levels [305.48963] relocated to 305.482; white collar classes relocated to office worker

.96513 and clerks .965137 in 305; Regional nationalism [320.549] relocated to 320.54; numbers [331.114224], [.11423], [.1143] relocated to 331.11422; groups of people [362.608] relocated to 362.69; [372.82] Home economics relocated to 372.37; and Chapbooks [398.5] relocated to 002 and chapbooks relating to a specific subject with the subject.

Languages

Pragmatics 401.45; speech perception 401.95; Corpus linguistics 410.188; Picture dictionaries 413.17; Maldivian languages 491.489; and Pahari languages 491.496 are the new numbers introduced in the schedules of languages. The class numbers which are revised and expanded include: 427.942 Geographic variations of English in England and Wales; 437.943 Geographic variations of German in Germany and neighboring central European countries; 447.944 Geographic variations of French in France and Monaco; 457.9 Geographic variations of Italian; and 467.946 Geographic variations of Spanish in Spain, Andorra, Gibraltar, Portugal.

Here also some numbers are relocated, and some are discontinued and relocated. These numbers are: Geographic variations of languages are discontinued and relocated from [427.1-.8] to 427.9421-.9428; [437.1-.6] to 437.9431-.9436; [439.8171-.8175] to 439.81794891-.81794895; [439.8272-.8274] to 439.8279482-.8279484; [447.1-.8] to 447.9441-.9448; [457.1-.8] to 457.9451-.9458; and many others. The provision of adding standard subdivisions to few languages is changed. Now only one zero is to be added instead of two zeros for the languages of Old Norse, Icelandic, Faroese; Hindi; Bulgarian and related South Slavic; Polish and related West Slavic; Tibetan and related Tibeto-Burman; and Thai and related Tai languages.

Natural sciences and mathematics

The schedule of natural sciences and mathematics has very limited changes. Certain new numbers introduced are 511.314 Modal logic; 511.317 Conditional logic; 511.318 Probabilistic logic; 514.746 Singularity theory; 515.882 Convex functions; 551.417 Wetland geomorphology; and 581.39 Age characteristics of plants. The only relocation is Trans-Neptunian objects 523.49 from 523.48. The discontinued and relocated numbers are: Meridional instruments [522.3] and Extra-meridional instruments [522.4] relocated to 522.2; and Sextants relocated to 527.0284. One zero is reduced while adding the standard subdivisions to Foundations of algebra 512.9. So, now standard subdivision numbers will be 512.901-.909 instead of 512.9001.9009.

Technology

In the schedule of Technology, a large number of new numbers have been introduced. Some of these are: 613.265 Raw food diet; 613.71489 Qi gong; 615.8514 Biofeedback therapy; 616.0475 Shock and multiple organ failure; 616.34473 Ulcerative colitis; 616.89147 Brief psychotherapy; 616.9693 Candidiasis; 618.29 Nonsurgical methods of abortion; 623.8282 Fishing boats; 624.238 Cable-stayed bridges; 636.08321 Animal hospitals; 641.8153 Crepes, pancakes, waffles; 659.1045 Use of image and themes in advertizing; 665.37 Biodiesel fuel; 684.162 Manufacturing of shelving; and 690.4 Specific parts of building.

Many relocations are also made in these classes. The class number for Connective tissue cells is relocated to 611.01826, Adipocytes to 611.018276, and Epithelial cells to 611.01876 from 611.0181; Local surface rail system using conventional (heavy) rail technology is relocated to 625.4 from 625.6; Pants (trousers) relocated to 646.436 from

646.433; Headscarves 687.19 relocated to 687.4; and headwear used as equipment in a specific sport is relocated to 688.7 from 687.4.

A number of class numbers are discontinued and relocated to other places. These are The class numbers [611.0183-.0186] are relocated to other places in 612; other hydraulic structures [627.92], [.922], and [.924] are relocated to 623.893, .8942, and .8944 respectively; [641.532] Brunches relocated to 641.52; [667.8] Japans and Japanning relocated to 667.75; [685.361], [.362], [.363], [.364], and [.367] Footwear for specific activities relocated to Ice-skates 688.7691, Roller skates 688.7621, Skateboards 688.7622, Snowshoes 688.7692, Skis 688.7693, and stilts 688.7.

Arts & recreation

Minimalism 709.04058; Use of solar energy 720.4724; Fountains as handicrafts 745.5946; Electronica 781.648; Beauty contests 791.66; Taekwondo 796.8157; Broomball 796.965; Water polo 797.252; Eventing 798.242; etc are the new numbers introduced in the schedules of Arts and recreation.

The number for Green technology 720.28 relocated to 720.47; Cloisters 726.69 relocated to 726.796; Architecture of agricultural buildings 725.37 relocated to 728.92; Groups of hunter 757.6 relocated to 758.979929; Photography of specific subjects by special kinds of photography relocated to 778.9 from 778.3; Stereoscopic photography and projection of specific subjects relocated to 778.9 from 778.4; and Third stream music tradition relocated to 781.68175 from 781.657.

The numbers which are discontinued and relocated are: [721.01-.03] Standard subdivisions of Architectural materials and structural elements relocated to 720.1-.3; [760.01-.03], [760.044], [760.05-.09], [760.0901-.0905], and

[760.092] relocated to 740.1-.3, 740.4, 740.5-.9, 740.901-.905, and 740.92 respectively; [771.33] Digital cameras relocated to 771.3; [771.47] Waste technology relocated to 771.40286; [775] Digital photography relocated to 771.44; [781.284] Polyphony relocated to 781.286; [796.78] Travel by private passenger automobile and [796.79] Travel by motor homes, recreational vehicles, trailers both relocated to 910.

Literature

Plagiarism 808.025; Toasts and after dinner speeches 808.512; Galician literature 869.9; Maldivian literature 891.489; Pahari literature 891.496 are the few new class numbers introduced in the schedules of literature. Two new instructions appeared under 808.8198 have made the provision of adding notation 05-09 from Table 5 to base number 808.8198 for Poetry for and by ethnic and national groups and under 808.8199 has made the provision of adding the numbers following -9 in notation 91-99 from Table 3C for Poetry for and by groups of people with specific attributes, residents of specific areas. Resultantly, the numbers like, [808.810081-.810088], [.810091-.810099] and other similar subdivisions of .82-.87 are discontinued and relocated to other places i.e. according to the above mentioned instructions. Another number discontinued and relocated to 894.57 is [894.55] Sami literatures.

History & geography

Historical periods of couple of countries have been revised and expanded in this edition of DDC. These countries are Italy, San Marino, Vatican City, Malta; and Vietnam. The historical periods of other countries are also expanded and new periods are included e.g. 947.0862 Administration of Vladimir Vladimirovich Putin; 954.0532 Prime minister ship of Manmohan Singh; 966.9055 Administration of Umaru Musa Yar'adua; 972.0842

Administration of Felipe Calderon Hinojosa; 985.0645 Administration of Alan Garcia; 994.071 Later part of prime minister ship of John Howard; etc.

A number of relocations are also made: Early history of Ireland for the period of 410-433 is relocated to 936.1502 from 941.501; Medieval history of Italy, San Marino, Vatican City, Malta relocated to 945.01 from 945.03; History of Moldova to ca. 640 relocated to 939.88 from 947.6; Early history to 358 of Indonesia and East Timor 959.8012 relocated to 959.8011; History of Ethiopia during 1991-1993 relocated to 963.0721 from 963.071; and many other numbers have been relocated. This all is a result of expansion of historical periods of various countries. Many numbers are discontinued and relocated to other places like: [939.47] relocated to 935.4, 935.5, and 953.02; [940-990:086914] relocated to 940-990:1; [959.8036], [.8038], [.8039] relocated to 959.8035, .8037, and .8041; [971.0187] relocated to 971.5017.

CONCLUSION

Though the credit of continuous revisions and modifications should not be taken from Decimal Classification Editorial Policy Committee, still there is a scope of improvement in Dewey Decimal Classification. The major areas are: i. The separation of Languages from Literature, ii. Separation of Geography and History from Social Sciences, iii. Area Table. The separation of Languages from the literature is a problem for the readers. In a large multi-storey library, even the floors at which the documents relating to Languages are different from that of Literature. Though, the users are more comfortable when both these classes are available side by side. In the similar fashion, there are great chances that a user of social science would also have some interest in History and Geography too. The same problem as of Languages and Literatures comes in the way of readers of large libraries exist here too. The notation for numbers of cities and states of countries other than USA and UK is not exhaustive one. In other words, we can say specifically that the numbers provided for the Asian countries are insufficient. For instance even the numbers for all the Districts of India is not covered in spite of its regular revisions.

REFERENCES

1. Dewey, Melvil. Dewey Decimal Classification and relative index. Edition 23. Dublin, OCLC, 2011.

3

Introduction to the Schedules

After going through chapter 1, you must be now able to make some simple class numbers. Let us start with examples of simple class numbers.

Internet Telephony	**004.695**
Class No.	004.695
Software	**005.3**
Class No.	005.3
Computer graphics	**006.6**
Class No.	006.6
Lighting for Library building	**022.7**
Class No.	022.7
Dewey Decimal Classification	**025.431**
Class No.	025.431
Hospital libraries	**027.662**
Class No.	027.662

Personnel management of Museums	**069.63**
Class No.	069.63
Photo Journalism	**070.49**
Class No.	070.49
Intelligence tests	**153.93**
Class No.	153.93
Psychology of married women	**155.645 3**
Class No.	155.645 3
Ethics of friendship	**177.62**
Class No.	177.62
Sikhism	**294.6**
Class No.	294.6
Ramayana	**294.592 2**
Class No.	294.592 2
Sociology of middle class	**305.55**
Class No.	305.55
Civil rights of young people	**323.352**
Class No.	323.352
Refugees	**325.21**
Class No.	325.21
Membership of labour unions	**331.873 2**
Class No.	331.873 2
National banks	**332.122 3**
Class No.	332.122 3
Legal systems	**340.5**
Class No.	340.5

Customs tax law	**343.056**
Class No.	343.056
Supreme Court	**347.732 6**
Class No.	347.732 6
Public administration of civil matters	**353.44**
Class No.	353.44
Forensic science	**363.25**
Class No.	363.25
Public secondary schools	**373.224**
Class No.	373.224
Export trade policy	**382.63**
Class No.	382.63
Real analysis	**515.8**
Class No.	515.8
Numerical integration	**518.54**
Class No.	518.54
Statistics	**519.5**
Class No.	519.5
Variable stars	**523.844**
Class No.	523.844
Dispersion of light	**535.4**
Class No.	535.4
Cyclic compounds	**547.5**
Class No.	547.5
Weather satellites	**551.635 4**
Class No.	551.635 4

Bioinorganic chemistry	**572.51**
Class No.	572.51
Poisonous plants	**581.659**
Class No.	581.659
Squirrels	**599.36**
Class No.	599.36
Pharmacy	**615.1**
Class No.	615.1
Disease of digestive system	**616.3**
Class No.	616.3
Lungs surgery	**617.542**
Class No.	617.542
Lasers engineering	**621.366**
Class No.	621.366
Tunnels engineering	**624.193**
Class No.	624.193
Irrigation Engineering	**627.52**
Class No.	627.52
Muskmelons crops	**635.611**
Class No.	635.611
Saddle horses	**636.12**
Class No.	636.12
Bee keeping	**638.1**
Class No.	638.1
Breakfast cooking	**641.52**
Class No.	641.52

Cost accounting	**657.42**
Class No.	657.42
Export marketing	**658.84**
Class No.	658.84
Petroleum technology	**665.5**
Class No.	665.5
Polyesters textiles	**677.474 3**
Class No.	677.474 3
Central heating engineering	**697.03**
Class No.	697.03
Monumental brass metalwork	**739.522**
Class No.	739.522
Binary form of music	**781.822 2**
Class No.	781.822 2
Taekwondo	**796.815 7**
Class No.	796.815 7
History of India under British rule	**954.03**
Class No.	954.03
20th century history of Canary islands	**964.908**
Class No.	964.908

Class numbers can also be made by following the various notes. Many notes have been elaborated in chapter 1. Now we will make some class numbers by following the notes.

CD-ROM storage disc	**004.565**
Optical storage	004.565

Note	Including CD-Rom, DVD, ...
Class No.	004.565
(This is an including note)	
Local Library	**027.5**
Government Library	027.5
Note	National, state, provincial, local
Class No.	027.5
(This is a scope note)	
Internet publishing	**070.579 73**
Web publications	070.579 73
Note	Class here Internet publishing
Class No.	070.579 73
(This is a class here note)	
Cross-cultural psychology	**155.8**
Emotions	155.8
Note	Class here cross-cultural psychology
Class No.	155.8
(This is a class here note)	
Ancient Eastern philosophy	**181**
Eastern philosophy	181
Note	Ancient, medieval, modern
Class No.	181
(This is a scope note)	
Hinayana Buddhism	**294.391**

Theravada Buddhism	294.391
Note	Variant names: Southern, Hinayana Buddhism
Class No.	294.391
(This is a variant name note)	
Home loan associations	**332.32**
Savings and loan associations	332.32
Note	Variant names: building and loan associations, ... Home loan associations, ...
Class No.	332.32
(This is a variant name note)	
Training of individual and units in Military	**355.5**
Military training	355.5
Note	Training of individual and units
Class No.	355.5
(This is a definition note)	
North American red squirrels	**599.363**
Tamiasciurus	599.363
Note	Variant names: North American red squirrels, chickarees
Class No.	599.363
(This is a variant name note)	
Maxima combinatorics	**511.66**
Extremal combinatorics	511.66

Note	Class here maxima, minima
Class No.	511.66
(This is a class here note)	
Trolleybus rail transit systems	**625.6**
Light rail transit systems	625.6
Note	Including trolleybus systems
Class No.	625.6
(This is an including note)	
Cocksfoot	**633.22**
Orchard grass	633.22
Note	Variant name: cocksfoot
Class No.	633.22
(This is a variant name note)	
Flat racing	**798.4**
Horse racing	798.4
Note	Class here flat racing
Class No.	798.4
(This is a class here note)	

These were the very simple notes. One note which I found a number of distance education students struggling with is an add note. If this note is taken as mathematical application, it is very simple to follow. In simple terms, an add note instruct the classifier to add certain number or part of it, from a range specified in this note. Let's look the format of add note and its mathematical step-by-step application.

If you have to classify a title "Mathematics libraries".

You have to take the following steps and your class number is ready. You will find a number 026 Libraries, archives, information centers devoted to specific subjects and disciplines. Under its subdivisions you will find .001-.999 Specific subjects and disciplines and below this there is an add note which reads as under:

Add to base number 026 notation 001-999

Follow the following steps:

Steps		Class numbers
Step 1	Note down the base number given in note	026
Step 2	Go to schedule and find a relevant number from the range specified in note e.g. 001 to 999	510 (Mathematics)
Step 3	Add (Join) this number to the base number	026+510
Step 4	Rewrite the number by omitting + sign and as per DDC rules	026.51

(**Note:** Here a dot is inserted after first three digits and the last zero is omitted because it was there only to complete the minimum three digits.)

More examples with somewhat more difficult add note.

1. Title: Hindu Temples

Go to 294.5 which is Hinduism and 294.51-.53 is Mythology, relations, doctrines, public worship and other practices and below to this is an add note.

Add to base number 294.5 the numbers following 20 in 201-203.

Follow the following steps:

Step 1.	Note the base number	294.5
Step 2.	Go to 201 to 203 in schedule and find a suitable number (Temples)	203.5
Step 3.	Omit the number written between the words **"following"** and **"in"** in the note (e.g. 20 in this note) from the number obtained at step 2	~~20~~3.5

Step 4.	Add (Join) the remaining number to the base number	294.5+3.5
Step 5.	Rewrite the number	294.535

2. Title: Raising of sheep for wool

636.3 is Sheep and goats and 636.31 is Sheep for specific purposes and below to this is an add note.

Add to base number 636.31 the numbers following 636.088 in 636.0882-636.0889.

Follow the following steps:

Step 1	Note the base number	636.31
Step 2	Go to 636.0882 to 636.0889 in schedule and find a suitable number (Animals raised for wool)	636.088 45
Step 3	Omit the number written between the words **"following"** and **"in"** in the note (e.g. 636.088 in this note) from the number obtained at step 2	~~636.088~~ 45
Step 4	Add (Join) the remaining number to the base number	636.31+45
Step 5	Rewrite the number	636.31 45

In the next few pages the class numbers made according to above formula are provided.

Classification of Organic Chemistry	**025.465 47**
Base Number	025.46
Instruction	Add to base number 025.46 notation 001-999
Organic chemistry	547
	=025.46+547
Class No.	025.465 47

Political parties libraries	**026.324 2**
Base Number	026
Instruction	Add to base number 026 notation 001-999

Political parties	324.2
	=026+324.2
Class No.	026.324 2
Tests for judo ability	**153.947 968 152**
Base Number	153.94
Instruction	Add to base number 153.94 notation 001-999
Judo	796.815 2
	=153.94+796.815 2
Class No.	153.947 968 152
Astrological analysis of cricket	**133.587 963 58**
Base Number	133.58
Instruction	Add to base number 133.58 notation 001-999
Cricket	796.358
	=133.58+796.358
Class No.	133.587 963 58
Psychology of deaf children	**155.451 2**
Base Number	155.45
Instruction	Add to base number 155.45 the numbers following 371.9 in 371.91-371.95
Deaf children	~~371.9~~12
	=155.45+12
Class No.	155.451 2
Sikh philosophy	**181.046**
Base Number	181.0

Instruction	Add to base number 181.0 the numbers following 29 in 294-299
Sikh	~~29~~4.6
	=181.0+46
Class No.	181.046

Ethics of homosexuality in Hinduism	**294.548 664**
Base Number	294.548 6
Instruction	Add to base number 294.5486 the numbers following 17 in 172-179
Ethics of homosexuality	~~17~~6.4
	=294.548 6+64
Class No.	294.548 664

Financial economics in Halakhah	**296.188 332**
Base Number	296.188
Instruction	Add to base number 296.188 notation 001-999
Financial economics	332
	=296.188 +332
Class No.	296.188 332

Public opinions of university librarians	**303.388 027 7**
Base Number	303.388
Instruction	Add to base number 303.388 notation from 001-999
University libraries	027.7

	=303.388+027.7
Class No.	303.388 027 7

Women dentists	**305.436 176**
Base Number	305.43
Instruction	Add to base number 305.43 notation 001-999
Dentists	617.6
	=305.43+617.6
Class No.	305.436 176

Industrial relations in Glass industry	**331.041 666 1**
Base Number	331.041
Instruction	Add to base number 331.041 notation 001-999
Glass industry	666.1
	=331.041+666.1
Class No.	331.041 666 1

Nuclear weapons as Military equipment	**355.825 119**
Base Number	355.82
Instruction	Add to base number 355.82 the numbers following 623.4 in 623.43-623.46
Nuclear weapons	~~623.4~~51 19
	=355.82+5119
Class No.	355.825 119

Teacher-Parent relations in primary schools	**372.110 3**
Base Number	372.1

Instruction	Add to base number 372.1 the numbers following 371 in 371.1-371.8
Teacher-Parent relations	~~371~~.103
	=372.1+103
Class No.	372.110 3
Costumes of gynecologists	**391.046 181**
Base Number	391.0
Instruction	Add to base number 391.0 the numbers following 390 in 390.1-390.4
Customs of people by occupation	~~390~~.4
Instruction	Add to base number 390.4 notation 001-999
Gynecologists	618.1
	=391.0+4+618.1
Class No.	391.046 181
Euclidean of line geometry	**516.218 3**
Base Number	516.21
Instruction	Add to base number 516.21 the numbers following 516.1 in 516.12-516.18
Line geometry	~~516.1~~83
	=516.21+83
Class No.	516.218 3
Astrophysics of Neutrons	**523.013 721 3**
Base Number	523.013

Instruction	Add to base number 523.013 the numbers following 536 in 536.1-536.7
Neutrons	~~539.~~721 3
	=523.013+721 3
Class No.	523.013 721 3

Orbit of Venus	**523.423**
Base Number (Venus*)	523.42
Instruction	Add to notation for each number identified by * the numbers following 523.3 in 523.31-523.33
Orbit	~~523.3~~3
	=523.42+3
Class No.	523.423

(Note here instruction is provided as foot note with * mark)

Dimensions of Jupiter satellites	**523.985 1**
Base Number	523.98
Instruction	Add to base number 523.98 the numbers following 523.4 in 523.43-523.48
Jupiter*	~~523.4~~5
Instruction	Add to notation for each number identified by * the numbers following 523.3 in 523.31-523.33
Dimensions	~~523.3~~1
	=523.98+5+1
Class No.	523.985 1

Hindu calendar	**529.324 5**
Base Number	529.32
Instruction	Add to base number 529.32 the numbers following 29 in 292-299
Hinduism	~~29~~4.5
	=529.32+45
Class No.	529.324 5

Thermal properties of plasmas	**530.442**
Base Number	530.44
Instruction	Add to base number 530.44 the numbers following 530.41 in 530.412-530.416
Thermal properties	~~530.41~~2
	=530.44+2
Class No.	530.442

Solid-state physics of ternary superconductors	**537.623 3**
Base Number	537.623
Instruction	Add to base number 537.623 the numbers following 537.622 in 537.6221-537.6226
Ternary superconductors	~~537.622~~ 3
	=537.623+3
Class No.	537.623 3

Acceleration of neutron particles	**539.737 3**
Base Number	539.737

Instruction	Add to base number 539.737 the numbers following 539.721 in 539.7211-539.7217
Neutron	~~539.721~~ 3
	=539.737+3
Class No.	539.737 3
Plasma chemistry	**541.042 4**
Base Number	541.042
Instruction	Add to base number 541.042 the numbers following 530.4 in 530.41-530.44
Plasma physics	~~530.4~~4
	=541.042+4
Class No.	541.042 4
Photochemistry of Sodium	**546.382 55**
Base Number (Sodium*)	546.382
Instruction	Add to each subdivision identified by * as follows:
Physical chemistry	5
Instruction	Add to base number 5 the numbers following 541.3 in 541.33-541.39
Photochemistry	~~541.3~~5
	=546.382+5+5
Class No.	546.382 55
Aromatic sulfide compounds	**547.661**
Base Number	547.6

Instruction	Add to base number 547.6 the numbers following 547.0 in 547.02-547.08
Sulfide	~~547.0~~61
	=547.6+61
Class No.	547.661

Minerals in Sedimentary rocks	**549.114 5**
Base Number	549.114
Instruction	Add to base number 549.114 the numbers following 552 in 552.1-552.5
Sedimentary rocks	~~552~~.5
	=549.114+5
Class No.	549.114 5

Variations in snow and snowfall over time	**551.578 43**
Base Number	551.578 4
Instruction	Add to base number 551.578 4 the numbers following 551.577 in 551.5771-551.5773
Variations over time	~~551.577~~ 3
	=551.578 4+3
Class No.	551.578 43

Paleontology of Quaternary period	**560.179**
Base Number	560.17
Instruction	Add to base number 560.17 the numbers following 551.7 in 551.71-551.79

Quaternary period	~~551.79~~
	=560.17+9
Class No.	560.179
Cryptozoic eon paleobotany	**561.111**
Base Number	561.11
Instruction	Add to base number 561.11 the numbers following 551.7 in 551.71-551.79
Cryptozoic eon	~~551.7~~1
	=561.11+1
Class No.	561.111
Fossil brown algae	**561.938**
Base Number	561.93
Instruction	Add to base number 561.93 the numbers following 579.8 in 579.82-579.89
Brown algae	~~579.88~~
	=561.93+8
Class No.	561.938
Paleontology of Mako sharks	**567.383**
Base Number	567.38
Instruction	Add to base number 567.38 the numbers following 597.3 in 597.33-597.39
Mako sharks	~~579.33~~
	=567.38+3
Class No.	567.383

Physiology of Asteroidea	**571.139 3**
Base Number	571.1
Instruction	Add to base number 571.1 the numbers following 59 in 590.1-599
Asteroidea	593.93
	=571.1+393
Class No.	571.139 3

Physiology of Roses	**571.237 3**
Base Number	571.2
Instruction	Add to base number 571.2 the numbers following 58 in 581-588
Rosa (Roses)	583.73
	=571.2+373
Class No.	571.237 3

Analytical biochemistry of iron	**572.517 36**
Base Number (Iron†)	572.517
Instruction	Except for modification shown under specific entries, add to each subdivision identified by † as follows:
Anatomy and application of specific process	33-39
To other processes	
Instruction	Add to 3 the numbers following 572.3 in 572.33-572.39
Analytical biochemistry	572.36

	=572.517+3+6
Class No.	572.517 36

(Note: Here instruction is provided through footnote with †mark)

Anatomy of bones	**573.762 733**
Base Number (Bones*)	573.76
Instruction	Except for modification shown under specific entries, add to each subdivision identified by * as follows:
Anatomy and general biological processes of muscles	273
Instruction	Add to 273 the numbers following 571 in 571.3-571.9
Anatomy	~~571~~.3
	=573.76+273+3
Class No.	573.762 733

(Note: Here instruction is provided through footnote with * mark)

Organisms characteristic of mountains	**578.753**
Base Number	578.7
Instruction	Add to base number 578.7 the numbers following 577 in 577.3-577.5
Mountain	~~577~~.53
	=578.7+53
Class No.	578.753

Reproductive adaptation of cactus	**583.561 46**
Base Number (Cactus*)	583.56

Instruction	Except for modification shown under specific entries, add to each subdivision identified by * as follows:
General topics of natural history of plants	1
Instruction	Add to base number 1 the numbers following 581 in 581.3-581.7
Reproductive adaptation	~~581~~.46
	=583.56+1+46
Class No.	583.561 46
Genetics of palm tree	**584.513 5**
Base Number (Palm*)	584.5
Instruction	Except for modification shown under specific entries, add to each subdivision identified by * as follows:
General topics of natural history of plants	1
Instruction	Add to base number 1 the numbers following 581 in 581.3-581.7
Genetics	~~581~~.35
	=584.5+1+35
Class No.	584.513 5
Family behavior of octopuses	**594.561 563**
Base Number (Octopuses*)	594.56
Instruction	Except for modification shown under specific entries,

add to each subdivision identified by * as follows:

General topics of natural history of animals — 1

Instruction — Add to base number 1 the numbers following 591 in 591.3-591.7

Family behavior — ~~591~~.563
=594.56+1+563

Class No. — 594.561 563

Seasonal adaptation of hippopotamuses — **599.635 143**

Base Number (hippopotamuses*) — 599.635

Instruction — Except for modification shown under specific entries, add to each subdivision identified by * as follows:

General topics of natural history of animals — 1

Instruction — Add to base number 1 the numbers following 591 in 591.3-591.7

Seasonal adaptation — ~~591~~.43
=599.635+1+43

Class No. — 599.635 143

Biochemistry of sulfur enzymes in humans — **612.015 155 4**

Base Number — 612.015 1

Instruction — add to base number 612.0151 the numbers following 572.7

	in 572.75-572.79
Enzymes	~~572.7~~
Instruction	Add to base number 572.7 the numbers following 572 in 572.5-572.8
Sulfur	~~572.7~~55 4
	=612.015 1+554
Class No.	612.015 155 42

Drugs derived from turmeric plants	**615.324 39**
Base Number	615.32
Instruction	Add to base number 615.32 the numbers following 58 in 583-587
Turmeric plants	~~58~~4.39
	=615.32+439
Class No.	615.324 39

Laboratory Diagnosis of Typhoid	**616.927 207 56**
Base Number (Typhoid *)	616.927 2
Instruction	Except for modification shown under specific entries, add to each subdivision identified by * as follows:
Diagnosis, prognosis, ...	075-079
Instruction	Add to 07 the numbers following 616.07 in 616.075-616.079
Laboratory Diagnosis	~~616.075~~ 6
	=616.927 2+07+56

Class No.	616.927 207 56
Treatment of asthma by thermotherapy	**616.238 063 2**
Base Number (Asthma*)	616.238
Instruction	Except for modification shown under specific entries, add to each subdivision identified by * as follows:
Other therapies	062-069
Instruction	Add to 06 the numbers following 615.8 in 615.82-615.89
Thermotherapy	~~615.8~~32
	=616.132+06+32
Class No.	616.238 063 2
Treatment of migraine by physiotherapy	**616.84912062**
Base Number (Migraine *)	616.849 12
Instruction	Except for modification shown under specific entries, add to each subdivision identified by * as follows:
Other therapies	062-069
Instruction	Add to 06 the numbers following 615.8 in 615.82-615.89
Physiotherapy	~~615.8~~2
	=616.849 12+06+2
Class No.	616.849 120 62

Surgical treatment of Cancer	**616.994 059**
Base Number (Cancer †)	616.994
Instruction	Except for modification shown under specific entries, add to each subdivision identified by † as follows:
Surgery	059
	=616.994 +059
Class No.	616.994 059

Occupational therapy of Lung Tuberclosis	**616.995 240 651 5**
Base Number	616.995
Instruction	Add to base number 616.995 the numbers following 611 in 611.2-611.9 and then add further as instructed under 616.1-616.9
Lung	~~611~~.24
Other therapies	062-069
Instruction	Add to 06 the numbers following 615.8 in 615.82-615.89
Occupational therapy	~~615.8~~515
	=616.995+24+06+515
Class No.	616.995 240 651 5

Intensive care for heart surgery	**617.412 028**
Base Number (Heart†)	617.412
Instruction	Except for modification

	shown under specific entries, add to each subdivision identified by † as follows:
Intensive care	028
	=617.412+028
Class No.	617.412 028
Plastic surgery of lips	**617.522 059 2**
Base Number (Oral region including lips *)	617.522
Instruction	Except for modification shown under specific entries, add to each subdivision identified by * as follows:
Plastic surgery	0592
	=617.522+059 2
Class No.	617.522 059 2
First aid for hips surgery	**617.581 026 2**
Base Number (Hips *)	617.581
Instruction	Except for modification shown under specific entries, add to each subdivision identified by * as follows:
First aid	026 2
	=617.581+026 2
Class No.	617.581 026 2
Treatment of disease of uterus by radiotherapy	**618.140 642**
Base Number (Diseases of uterus *)	618.14

Instruction	Except for modification shown under specific entries, add to each subdivision identified by * as follows:
Radiotherapy	064 2
	=618.14+064 2
Class No.	618.140 642
Diagnosis of Alzheimer among old age patients	**618.976 831 075**
Base Number	618.976
Instruction	Add to base number 618.976 the numbers following 616 in 616.1-616.9
Alzheimer *	~~616~~.831
Instruction	Except for modification shown under specific entries, add to each subdivision identified by * as follows:
Pathology	07
Instruction at 075-079	Add to 07 the numbers following 616.07 in 616.075-616.079
Diagnosis	~~616.07~~5
	=618.976+831+07+5
Class No.	618.976 831 075
Optical Diagnosis of cerebral palsy among children	**618.928 360 754 5**
Base Number (.921-.929)	618.92
Instruction	Add to base number 618.92 the numbers following 616 in

	616.1-616.9
Cerebral palsy *	~~616~~.836
Instruction	Except for modification shown under specific entries, add to each subdivision identified by * as follows:
Pathology	07
Instruction at 075-079	Add to 07 the numbers following 616.07 in 616.075-616.079
Optical diagnosis	~~616.07~~5 45 =618.92+836+07+545
Class No.	618.928 360 754 5
Treatment of Cholera among children	**618.929 320 6**
Base Number	618.92
Instruction	Add to base number 618.92 the numbers following 616 in 616.1-616.9
Cholera *	~~616~~.932
Instruction	Except for modification shown under specific entries, add to each subdivision identified by * as follows:
Treatment	06
	=618.92+932+06
Class No.	618.929 320 6
Interior Lighting in school library building	**621.322 782 8**

Base Number	621.322
Instruction	Add to base number 621.322 the numbers following 72 in 725-728
Library building	~~72~~7.82
Instruction	Add to base number ~~72~~7.82 the numbers following 027 in 027.1-027.8
School library	~~027~~.8
	=621.322+782+8
Class No.	621.322 782 8

Design of Power-driven ships	**623.812 044**
Base Number (Design of general crafts)	623.812 04
Instruction	Add to base number 623.8120 the numbers following 623.820 in 623.8202-623.8205
Power-driven ships	~~623.820~~ 4
	=623.812 04+4
Class No.	623.812 044

Models of rocket planes	**629.133 138**
Base Number (Models and miniatures)	629.133 1
Instruction	Add to base number 629.132 52 the numbers following 629.133 3 in 629.133 33-629.133 38
Rocket planes	~~629.133~~ 38
	=629.133 1+38
Class No.	629.133 138

Plant injuries by Scorpion flies	**632.744**
Base Number (Insect pests)	632.7
Instruction	Add to base number 632.7 the numbers following 595.7 in 595.72-595.79
Scorpion flies	~~595.7~~44 =632.7+44
Class No.	632.744

Crop rotation of Barley	**633.168 2**
Base Number (Barley *)	633.16
Instruction	Except for modification shown under specific entries, add to each subdivision identified by * as follows:
Special cultivation methods	8
Instruction	Add to 8 the numbers following 631.58 in 631.581-631.587
Crop rotation	~~631.58~~2 =633.16+8+2
Class No.	633.168 2

Green manures for Guavas	**634.421 897 4**
Base Number (Guavas *)	634.421
Instruction	Except for modification shown under specific entries, add to each subdivision identified by * as follows:
Fertilizers, soil conditions, growth regulators	89

Instruction	Add to 89 the numbers following 631.8 in 631.81-631.89
Green manures	~~631.8~~74
	=634.421+89+74
Class No.	634.421 897 4

Control of Bird lice in groundnut crops	**635.659 697 57**
Base Number (groundnut *)	635.659 6
Instruction	Except for modification shown under specific entries, add to each subdivision identified by * as follows:
Injuries, disease, pests	9
Instruction	Add to 9 the numbers following 632 in 632.1-632.9
Insect pests	~~632~~.7
Instruction	Add to base number ~~632~~.7 the numbers following 595.7 in 595.72-595.79
Bird lice	~~595.7~~57
	=635.615+9+7+57
Class No.	635.659 697 57

Harvesting of flowering plants	**635.915 5**
Base Number (flowering plants)	635.91
Instruction	Add to base number 635.91 the numbers following 631 in 631.2-631.8

Harvesting	~~631~~.55 =635.91+55
Class No.	635.915 5
Artificial insemination of dogs	**636.108 245**
Base Number (Dogs)	636.70
Instruction	Add to base number 636.70 the numbers following 636.0 in 636.001-636.08
Artificial insemination	~~636.0~~82 45 =636.70+824 5
Class No.	636.708 245
Rearing of Cattles for milk	**636.208 842**
Base Number (Cattles)	636.20
Instruction	Add to base number 636.20 the numbers following 636.0 in 636.001-636.08
Animals raised for eggs and milk	~~636.0~~88 42 =636.20+884 2
Class No.	636.208 842
Treatment of virus disease in sheep	**636.308 969 106**
Base Number (Sheep and goats)	636.30
Instruction	Add to base number 636.30 the numbers following 636.0 in 636.001-636.08
Veterinary medicine	~~636.0~~89

Instruction	Add to base number 636.089 the numbers following 61 in 610-618
Virus disease*	~~61~~6.91
Instruction	Except for modification shown under specific entries, add to each subdivision identified by * as follows:
Treatment	06
	=636.30+89+691+06
Class No.	636.308 969 106
Hunting of penguins	**639.128 47**
Base Number (Hunting of specific kinds of birds)	639.128
Instruction	Add to base number 639.128 the numbers following 598 in 598.3-598.9
Penguins	~~598.~~47
	=639.128+47
Class No.	639.128 47
Cooking of rice	**641.631 8**
Base Number	641.6
Instruction	Add to base number 641.6 the numbers following 63 in 633-637
Rice	~~63~~3.18
	=641.6+318
Class No.	641.631 8
Construction of tops for women	**646.435 04**

Base Number (Shirts, blouses, tops *)	646.435
Instruction	Add to each subdivision identified by * as follows:
Clothing for ..., men, women, children	01-06
Instruction	Add to 0 the numbers following 646.40 in 646.401-646.406
Women	~~646.404~~
	=646.435+0+4
Class No.	646.435 04
Child rearing of siblings	**649.143**
Base Number	649.14
Instruction	Add to base number 649.14 the numbers following 155.44 in 155.442-155.446
Siblings	~~155.443~~
	=649.14+3
Class No.	649.143
Office services in yarn textiles	**651.967 702 862**
Base Number	651.9
Instruction	Add to base number 651.9 notation 001-999
Yarn textile	677.028 62
	=651.9+677 028 62
Class No.	651.967 702 862
Incentives for senior executives	**658.407 142**

Base Number	658.407
Instruction	Add to base number 658.407 the numbers following 658.3 in 658.31-658.38
Incentives	~~658.3~~14 2
	=658.407+142
Class No.	658.407 142

Quality controls for seafood	**664.949 7**
Base Number	664.949
Instruction	Add to base number 664.949 the numbers following 664.0 in 664.06-664.09
Quality control	~~664.0~~7
	=664.949+7
Class No.	664.949 7

Knitting of silk for textiles	**677.392 45**
Base Number	677.39
Instruction	Add to base number 677.39 the numbers following 677.028 in 677.0282-677.0287
Knitting	~~677.028~~ 245
	=677.39+245
Class No.	677.392 45

Architecture of building for management schools	**727.465 8**
Base Number	727.4
Instruction	Add to base number 727.4 notation 001-999

Management	658
	=727.4+658
Class No.	727.465 8

Functionalism in modern sculpture	**735.230 42**
Base Number	735.230 4
Instruction	Add to base number 735.230 4 the numbers following 709.040 in 709.0401-709.0407
Functionalism	~~709.040~~ 2
	=735.230 4+2
Class No.	735.230 42

Paintings of Hindu Gods	**758.929 452 11**
Base Number	758.9
Instruction	Add to base number 758.9 notation 001-999
Hinduism	294.5
Instruction	Add to base number 294.5 the numbers following 20 in 201-203
Gods	~~20~~2.11
	=758.9+294.5+211
Class No.	758.929 452 11

Photography of marine scenes	**778.937**
Base Number	778.9
Instruction	Add to base number 778.9 the numbers following 704.94 in 704.942-704.949

Marine scenes	~~704.94~~ 37
	=778.9+37
Class No.	778.937
Recording of Sikh sacred music	**781.746 49**
Base Number	781.7
Instruction	Add to base number 781.7 the numbers following 29 in 294-299; then add further as follows:
Sikhism	~~29~~4.6
Instruction	Add to base number 0 the numbers following 781 in 781.1-781.6
Recording of music	~~781~~.49
	=781.7+46+49
Class No.	781.746 49
Orchestra with friction drums	**784.269 8**
Base Number	784.2
Instruction	Add to base number 784.2 the numbers following 78 in 786-788
Friction drums	~~78~~6.98
	=784.2+698
Class No.	784.269 8
Sheep hunting as a game	**799.259 649**
Base Number	799.25
Instruction	Add to base number 799.25

	the numbers following 59 in 592-599
Sheep	599.649
	=799.25+964 9
Class No.	799.259 649

WORKS OF LAW

In the preceding pages we have dealt with all the schedules except 400 499, 340-349, 800-899 and 900-999. The schedule of languages i.e. 400 499 is dealt in chapter 7 and schedule of literature i.e. 800-899 is dealt in chapter 6. The schedules of law 340-349 and 900-999 are being dealt in the next few pages. There is a definite reason for dealing with these schedules separately. The reason is the procedure of making class number from these schedules is little bit different. Let us try it.

The class numbers of Works of law in DDC are made under 340 and its subdivisions. The works of law can be divided into two categories.

1. Works on International law
2. Works on law other than international law

The works on/and about international law are to be classified under 341. In this category class numbers can be made of treaties, disputes and conflicts among countries, war, etc. Let us take first of all some examples of International law.

Japanese treaties	**341.026 452**
Base Number	341.026 4
Instruction	Add to base number 341.026 4 notation 1-9 from Table 2
Japan (Table 2)	-52
	=341.026 4+52

Class No.	341.026 452
Treaties between India and USA	**341.026 654 073**
Base Number	341.026 6
Instruction	Add to base number 341.026 6 notation 3-9 from Table 2; then add 0 and again add notation 3-9 from Table 2.
India (Table 2)	-54
Indicator digit	0
USA (Table 2)	-73
	=341.026 6+54+0+73
Class No.	341.026 654 073
Air space Treaties between UK and Australia	**341.460 266 410 94**
Base Number (Air space†)	341.46
Instruction	Except for modification shown under specific entries, add to each subdivision identified by † as follows:
Text of treaties	0261-0266
Instruction	Add to base number 026 the numbers following 341.026 in 341.0261-341.0266
Bilateral treaties	~~341.026~~ 6
Instruction	Add to base number ~~341.026~~ 6 notation 3-9 from Table 2; then add 0 and again add notation 3-9 from Table 2.

UK (Table 2)	-41
Indicator digit	0
Australia (Table 2)	-94
	=341.46+026+6+41+0+94
Class No.	341.460 266 410 94
Disarmament Treaties between UK and USA	**341.733 026 641 073**
Base Number (Disarmament†)	341.733
Instruction	Except for modification shown under specific entries, add to each subdivision identified by † as follows:
Text of treaties	0261-0266
Instruction	Add to base number 026 the numbers following 341.026 in 341.0261-341.0266
Bilateral treaties	~~341.026~~ 6
Instruction	Add to base number ~~341.026~~ 6 notation 3-9 from Table 2; then add 0 and again add notation 3-9 from Table 2.
UK (Table 2)	-41
Indicator digit	0
USA (Table 2)	-73
	=341.733+026+6+41+0+73
Class No.	341.733 026 641 073

Class numbers for law of specific jurisdictions and areas are built from following five elements:

1. The base number indicating law 34

2. A digit indicating specific branch of law, original materials, or comprehensive works as follows:

Constitutional and administrative law	2
Military, defense, public property, public finance, tax, trade, industrial law	3
Labor, social service, education, cultural law	4
Criminal law	5
Private law	6
Procedure and courts	7
Laws , regulations, cases not limited to a specific branch	8
Comprehensive works	9

3. The facet indicator 0

4. One or more digits indicating a subject subordinate to specific branch of law or type of original material

For example: Courts	1
Trials	7

5. Notation from table 2 indicating the jurisdiction or area

   For example: India -54

To show comprehensive works on a specific jurisdiction or area in modern world, the elements are to be arranged as under:

1. Base number
2. Digit indicating comprehensive works
3. Jurisdiction or area

For example:

Law of India	**349.54**
Base Number	34
Comprehensive works	9

India (Table 2)	-54
	=34+9+54
Class No.	349.54

To show a specific branch, a specific subject, or a kind of original material, arrange the elements as follows:

1. Base number
2. Branch of law
3. Jurisdiction or area
4. Facet indicator (0)
5. Subordinate subject in branch of law

For example:

Income tax law of India	**343.540 52**
Base Number	34
Branch of law	3
India (Table 2)	-54
Facet indicator	0
Income tax	52
	=34+3+54+0+52
Class No.	343.540 52

Generally this is the way of classifying works on law other than international law. However, there are three other preferred optional procedures, which are explained below. The examples in this book have been solved according to above procedure.

Option 1. To give local emphasis and a shorter notation to law of a specific jurisdiction or area, the elements can be arranged as under:

1. Base number
2. Branch of law
3. Facet indicator (0)
4. Subordinate subject in the branch of law

(For law of a jurisdiction subordinate to the emphasized jurisdiction or area, insert between the branch of law and facet indicator the notation indicating the subordinate jurisdiction)

The above class number will be like this:

Income tax law of India	**343.052**
Base Number	34
Branch of law	3
Facet indicator	0
Income tax	52
	=34+3+0+52
Class No.	343.052

(Please note here to show subordinate jurisdiction of an area with regular notation from Table 2, derive the notation by dropping from the area number for subordinate jurisdiction all digits that apply to preferred jurisdiction. For example, drop area number for India -54 from area number for Haryana -54558 to obtain notation 558, which is to be used for Haryana. Thus the class number for Income tax law in Haryana is 343.558 052.

Option 2. To give preferred treatment to jurisdictions in general, arrange elements as follows:

1. Base number
2. Jurisdiction or area
3. Facet indicator (0)
4. Branch of law
5. Subordinate subject in the branch of law

The same class number will be like this:

Income tax law of India	**345.403 52**
Base Number	34
India (Table 2)	54

Facet indicator	0
Branch of law	3
Income tax	52
	=34+54+0+3+52
Class No.	345.403 52

Option 3. To give preferred treatment to branch of law and its subordinate subjects, the elements can also be arranged as follows:

1. Base number
2. Branch of law
3. Subordinate subject in the branch of law
4. Facet indicator (0)
5. Jurisdiction or area

The above class number will become like this now:

Income tax law of India	**343.520 54**
Base Number	34
Branch of law	3
Income tax	52
Facet indicator	0
India (Table 2)	54
	=34+3+52+0+54
Class No.	343.520 54

In this way any book on law (other than International law) may have four different class numbers according to the same edition of DDC. Hence classifier has to decide as to which of the above procedures is suitable for his/her library. However, students can assign class numbers to the titles in the examination according to any of the above four procedures. In this book the very first procedure has been followed. Let us look other class numbers of law other than international law.

Legislative law of Canada	**342.710 5**
Base Number	34
Branch of law	2
Canada (Table 2)	71
Facet indicator	0
Legislative branch of Govt.	5
	=34+2+71+0+5
Class No.	342.710 5

Court decisions on abortion in China	**342.510 840 264 3**
Base Number	34
Branch of law	2
China (Table 2)	51
Facet indicator	0
Abortion*	84
Instruction	Except for modification shown under specific entries, add to each subdivision identified by * as follows:
Court decisions	026 43
	=34+2+51+0+84+026 43
Class No.	342.510 840 264 3

Regulations on rural development in Iraq	**343.567 074 502 63**
Base Number	34
Branch of law	3
Iraq (Table 2)	567
Facet indicator	0
Rural development *	745

Instruction	Except for modification shown under specific entries, add to each subdivision identified by * as follows:
Regulations	026 3
	=34+3+567+0+745+026 3
Class No.	343.567 074 502 63

Legal reports on customs tax law in Argentina	**343.820 560 264 2**
Base Number	34
Branch of law	3
Argentina (Table 2)	82
Facet indicator	0
Customs tax*	56
Instruction	Except for modification shown under specific entries, add to each subdivision identified by * as follows:
Legal reports	026 42
	=34+3+82+0+56+026 42
Class No.	343.820 560 264 2

Advisory opinions of attorney-general regarding welfare services to rape victims in Tasmania	**344.946 032 883 026 5**
Base Number	34
Branch of law	4
Tasmania (Table 2)	946
Facet indicator	0

Social welfare and service	.0321-.0328
Instruction	Add to base number 344.032 the numbers following 362 in 362.1-362.8; then add further as instructed under 342-347
Rape victims	362.883
Advisory opinions of attorney-general	026 5
	=34+4+946+0+32+883+026 5
Class No.	344.946 032 883 026 5

Administrative regulations for environmental protection in Italy	**344.450 636 370 263 6**
Base Number	34
Branch of law	4
Italy (Table 2)	45
Facet indicator	0
Specific kinds of public works	.0601-.06999
Instruction	Add to base number 344.06 notation 001-999; then ass further as instructed under 342-347
Environmental protection	363.7
Administrative regulations	026 36
	=34+4+45+0+6+363.7+026 36
Class No.	344.450 636 702 636

Statements of witnesses in phishing in Turkey	**345.561 363 370 363 6**

Base Number	34
Branch of law	5
Turkey (Table 2)	561
Facet indicator	0
Crimes *	2
Instruction	Add to base number 345.02 the numbers following 364.1 in 364.13-364.18
Phishing	~~364.1~~63 2
Instruction	Except for modification shown under specific entries, add to each subdivision identified by * as follows:
Statements of witnesses	026 2
	=34+5+561+0+2+632+026 2
Class No.	345.561 026 320 262

Digest of Copyright law in Fiji	**346.961 104 820 264 8**
Base Number	34
Branch of law	6
Fiji (Table 2)	961 1
Facet indicator	0
Copyright *	482
Instruction	Except for modification shown under specific entries, add to each subdivision identified by * as follows:
Digest	026 48
	=34+6+9611+0+482+026 48
Class No.	346.961 104 820 264 8

Fees for legal professional services in High Courts of Australia	**347.940 335 72**
Base Number	34
Branch of law	7
Australia (Table 2)	94
Facet indicator	0
High courts †	33
Instruction	Add to each subdivision identified by † as follows:
Specific topics of procedure	51-57
Instruction	Add to 5 the numbers following 347.05 in 347.051-347.057
Fees for legal	~~347.05~~7 2
professional services	=34+7+94+0+33+5+72
Class No.	347.940 335 72

WORKS OF GENERAL HISTORY, GEOGRAPHY AND BIOGRAPHY

The term "General History" is used here intentionally because the historical and geographical treatment of specific discipline or subject should be classified under the discipline or subject concerned. For example: history of Libraries, in Library science; Social history, in Social science; Economic history, in Economics; etc. In the very beginning of the schedule of History there is an instruction in this regard. The instruction reads as:

"Class history and geographic treatment of a specific subject with the subject, plus notation 09 from Table 1, e.g. history and geographic treatment of natural sciences 509, of economic situations and conditions 330.9, of purely political situations and conditions 320.9, history of military science 355.009."

The notation 900.1-9 is used for standard subdivisions of history and geography whereas 901 to 908 is used for standard subdivisions of history, and 909 is devoted to World history. Hence General history of the world is to be classified under 909. Under 909 there is a special provision of making class numbers of history of ethnic and national groups. Let us try some examples:

15th Century World History	**909.4**
Class No.	909.4
21st Century World History	**909.83**
Class No.	909.83
World History of Hakkas	**909.049 517**
Base Number	909.04
Instruction	Add to base number 909.04 notation 1-9 from Table 5
Hakkas (Table 5)	-951 7
	=909.04+951 7
Class No.	909.049 517
World History of Norwegians in 13th century	**909.043 982 02**
Base Number	909.04
Instruction	Add to base number 909.04 notation 05-9 from Table 5; then add 0 and to the result add the numbers following

	909 in 909.1-909.8
Norwegians (Table 5)	-398 2
13th century	~~909~~.2
	=909.04+398 2+0+2
Class No.	909.043 982 02

World History of Punjabis in 18th Century	**909.049 121 07**
Base Number	909.04
Instruction	Add to base number 909.04 notation 05-9 from Table 5; then add 0 and to the result add the numbers following 909 in 909.1-909.8
Punjabis (Table 5)	-912 1
18th century	~~909~~.7
	=909.04+912 1+0+7
Class No.	909.049 121 07

The schedule of 910 to 919 is devoted to Geography and travel. The works of geography of any specific continents, countries, localities in modern world can be classified under 913 to 919. There is an instruction below 913-919 to this effect. The instruction reads as under:

Add to base number 91 notation 3-9 from Table 2; then add further as follows:

Examples are provided below:

Geography of Haryana	**915.455 8**
Base Number	91
Instruction	Add to base number 91 notation 3-9 from Table 2
Haryana (Table 2)	-545 58

	=91+545 58
Class No.	915.455 8

Physical Geography of New Jersey	**917.490 2**
Base Number	91
Instruction	Add to base number 91 notation 3-9 from Table 2
New Jersey (Table 2)	-749
Physical Geography	02
	=91+749+02
Class No.	917.490 2

(Notation 02 is taken from table under 913-919)

Travel in Kashmir during Manmohan Singh's prime ministership	**915.460 453 2**
Base Number	91
Instruction	Add to base number 91 notation 3-9 from Table 2
Kashmir (Table 2)	-546
Travel	04
Instruction	Add to 04 the historical period numbers following 0 that appear in subdivisions of 930-990
Manmohan Singh's Prime Ministership	.053 2 =91+546+04+532
Class No.	915.460 453 2

Facilities for Travelers in New Zealand during Dominion period	**919.306 13**

Base Number	91
Instruction	Add to base number 91 notation 3-9 from Table 2
New Zealand (Table 2)	-93
Facilities for Travelers	061
Instruction	Add to 061 the historical period numbers following 0 that appear in subdivisions of 930-990
Dominion period	.93
	=91+93+061+3
Class No.	919.306 13

The schedule of 920 to 929 is devoted to Biography, genealogy, insignia but only 920 and 929 are used for General Biography and genealogy, names, insignia respectively. The rest numbers 921-928 are the optional numbers. There is a specific instruction right at the beginning of 920. The instruction reads as under:

Class biography of persons associated with a specific subject with the subject, plus notation 092 from Table 1.

For example:

Biography of Melvil Dewey	025.431 092
Base Number (For DDC)	025.431
Biography (Table 1)	-092
	=025.431+92
Class No.	020.92

However, DDC 23 provides three other options for classifying the works of biographies. These are:

Option A: For biography of people associated with a specific subject, use subdivisions identified by *, then for each number identified by †, add notation 3-9 from Table 2.

Under this provision the numbers from 920.1 to 928 have been provided for the biographies of specific subjects. These numbers have been shown as optional numbers by footnote. The major drawback of this option is the separation of works of biographies from other documents on the same subject. The use of biographies of a given subject is much expected by the users of that subject.

Option B: Class individual biography in 92 or B; class collected biography in 92 or 920 undivided.

Use of this option also invites the same drawbacks.

Option C: Class individual biography of men in 920.71; Class individual biography of women in 920.72.

Therefore, all the works of biography of persons relating to a subject should be classified under that subject by using notation 092 from Table 1. Only general biographies should be classified under 920. Some examples are given below:

Biography of 19th century persons	**920.009 034**
Base Number	920.009 0
Instruction	Add to base number 920.0090 the numbers following -090 in notation 090 1-090 5 from Table 1
19th Century (Table 1)	-~~090~~ 34 =920.009 0+34
Class No.	920.009 034

Biography of Urban persons	**920.009 173 2**
Base Number	920.009 1
Instruction	Add to base number 920.0091

	the numbers following -1 in notation 11-19 from Table 2
Urban (Table 2)	-173 2
	=920.009 1+732
Class No.	920.009 173 2

Biography of Marathas	**920.009 291 461**
Base Number	920.0092
Instruction	Add to base number 920.009 2 notation 05-9 from Table 5
Marathas (Table 5)	-914 61
	=920.009 2+914 61
Class No.	920.009 291 461

Biography of persons resident in Peru	**920.085**
Base Number	920.0
Instruction	Add to base number 920.0 notation 3-9 from Table 2
Peru (Table 2)	-85
	=920.0+85
Class No.	920.085

The schedule from 930 to 999 is devoted to History of Ancient world; of specific continents, countries, localities; of extraterrestrial worlds. An add note is given at 930-990 to make the class number of works of General history.

The examples are illustrated in the next few pages.

History of India during Babur	**954.025 2**
Base Number	9
Instruction	Add to base number 9

	notation 3-9 from Table 2; then add further as follows:
India (Table 2)	-54
Historical periods	01-09
Instruction	Add to 0 the period division numbers following 0 from the appropriate continent, country, locality in 930-990
Babur Period	-0252
	=9+54+0+252
Class No.	954.025 2

Twentieth Century Chinese History	**951.05**
Base Number	9
Instruction	Add to base number 9 notation 3-9 from Table 2; then add further as follows:
China (Table 2)	-51
Historical periods	01-09
Instruction	Add to 0 the period division numbers following 0 from the appropriate continent, country, locality in 930-990
20th Century	-05
	=9+52+0+5
Class No.	952.05

History of Ethiopian war	**963.043**
Base Number	9
Instruction	Add to base number 9 notation 3-9 from Table 2; then

	add further as follows:
Ethiopia (Table 2)	-63
Historical periods	01-09
Instruction	Add to 0 the period division numbers following 0 from the appropriate continent, country, locality in 930-990
Ethiopian war	-043
	=9+63+0+43
Class No.	963.043

Second republic history of Brazil	**981.06**
Base Number	9
Instruction	Add to base number 9 notation 3-9 from Table 2; then add further as follows:
Brazil (Table 2)	-81
Historical periods	01-09
Instruction	Add to 0 the period division numbers following 0 from the appropriate continent, country, locality in 930-990
20th Century	-06
	=9+81+0+6
Class No.	981.06

All these numbers can be assigned directly from the schedule also, but the procedure is same. However, the numbers for history of U S is an exception and the notation for period of history is added directly without a zero. The reason is very simple that the numbers for states of Unites states have been dealt separately in 974-979. The zero divisions have been used for standard subdivisions. For example:

Diplomatic history of United States	**973.32**
Base Number	9
Instruction	Add to base number 9 notation 3-9 from Table 2; then add further as follows:
United States (Table 2)	-73
Diplomatic history	.32
	=9+73+32
Class No.	973.32

Let us now try some examples of class numbers of various states of countries other than United States.

History of Haryana during 21st century	**954.558 053 2**
Base Number	9
Instruction	Add to base number 9 notation 3-9 from Table 2; then add further as follows:
Haryana (Table 2)	-545 58
Historical periods	01-09
Instruction	Add to 0 the period division numbers following 0 from the appropriate continent, country, locality in 930-990
21st Century	-053 2
	=9+545 58+0+532
Class No.	954.558 053 2

History of Gujarat during 17th century	**954.750 258**

Base Number	9
Instruction	Add to base number 9 notation 3-9 from Table 2; then add further as follows:
Gujarat (Table 2)	-547 5
Historical periods	01-09
Instruction	Add to 0 the period division numbers following 0 from the appropriate continent, country, locality in 930-990
17th Century	-025 8
	=9+547 5+0+258
Class No.	954.750 258

Twentieth century history of Tasmania **994.604**

Base Number	9
Instruction	Add to base number 9 notation 3-9 from Table 2; then add further as follows:
Tasmania (Table 2)	-946
Historical periods	01-09
Instruction	Add to 0 the period division numbers following 0 from the appropriate continent, country, locality in 930-990
20th Century	-04
	=9+946+0+4
Class No.	994.604

History of Delhi under Mogul empire **954.560 25**

Base Number	9
Instruction	Add to base number 9 notation 3-9 from Table 2; then add further as follows:
Delhi (Table 2)	-545 6
Historical periods	01-09
Instruction	Add to 0 the period division numbers following 0 from the appropriate continent, country, locality in 930-990
Mogul empire	-025
	=9+545 6+0+25
Class No.	954.560 25

History of Sindh under Mohammad Ali Jinnah **954.918 042**

Base Number	9
Instruction	Add to base number 9 notation 3-9 from Table 2; then add further as follows:
Sindh (Table 2)	-549 18
Historical periods	01-09
Instruction	Add to 0 the period division numbers following 0 from the appropriate continent, country, locality in 930-990
Administration of Mohammad Ali Jinnah	-042 =9+549 18+0+42
Class No.	954.918 042

History of Edo state during Nigerian Civil war **966.932 052**

Base Number	9
Instruction	Add to base number 9 notation 3-9 from Table 2; then add further as follows:
Edo state (Table 2)	-669 32
Historical periods	01-09
Instruction	Add to 0 the period division numbers following 0 from the appropriate continent, country, locality in 930-990
Period of Nigerian Civil war	-052
	=9+669 32+0+52
Class No.	966.932 052

History of Alessandria under Napoleon	**945.140 82**
Base Number	9
Instruction	Add to base number 9 notation 3-9 from Table 2; then add further as follows:
Alessandria (Table 2)	-451 4
Historical periods	01-09
Instruction	Add to 0 the period division numbers following 0 from the appropriate continent, country, locality in 930-990
Napoleonic period	-082
	=9+451 4+0+82
Class No.	945.140 82

History of West Sussex under Elizabeth-I	**942.260 55**

Base Number	9
Instruction	Add to base number 9 notation 3-9 from Table 2; then add further as follows:
West Sussex (Table 2)	-422 6
Historical periods	01-09
Instruction	Add to 0 the period division numbers following 0 from the appropriate continent, country, locality in 930-990
Elizabeth-I	.055
	=9+422 6+0+55
Class No.	942.260 55

4

Use of Table 1: Standard Subdivisions

As mentioned in the chapter1, 6 tables have been provided in DDC 23. The first table contains standard subdivisions. A standard subdivision represents a recurring physical form (such as an encyclopedia, periodical, or index) or approach (such as history or research) and thus is applicable to any subject or discipline that covers or approximates the whole of the meaning of the number. These standard subdivisions are like common isolates in colon classification although these are not hundred percent same. The provision of standard subdivisions was made in the second edition of DDC published in 1885 for the first time and since then these have been called differently in different editions of DDC. The various names used for standard subdivisions are mention in the below table:

Sr. No.	Edition/s	Name used for standard subdivisions
1	2nd to 12th	Form Divisions
2	13th	Common Subdivisions
3	14th	Uniform Subdivisions
4	15th & 16th	Form Divisions
5	17th to 23rd	Standard Subdivisions

RULES FOR ADDING STANDARD SUBDIVISIONS

A standard subdivision is never used alone, but may be used as required with any regular schedule number, e.g. Dictionary (03 notation in table 1) of Economics (330): 330.03. While adding the standard subdivisions from table 1 following rules must be followed.

Standard subdivisions can be added to any number in the schedule (without waiting for invitation to add standard subdivisions) unless there is a specific instruction to the contrary. For example:

Encyclopedia of Child Psychology	**155.403**
Child Psychology	155.4
Encyclopedia	-03 (ss)
	= 155.4+03
Class No.	155.403

(Please note that the number for Child psychology is 155.4 in the schedule and notation for encyclopedia (-03) is standard subdivision (ss) provided in table 1. We added a standard subdivision without waiting for an invitation or instruction to add standard subdivision.)

The most important caveat with respect to standard subdivisions is that they are added only for works that cover or approximate the whole of the subject of the number. For example, a work on black widow spiders of California should be classed in the number for spiders

595.44 (not 595.4409794). Here California should not be specified because black widow spiders do not approximate the whole universe of spiders in California, and there is not a specific number available for black widows.

If the ultimate class number is a main class or a division i.e. ends with one zero or two zeroes, the zeroes filling the vacant space are to be removed before adding a standard subdivision; and the digits are reshuffled after that the dot is put after the first three digits. For example:

Encyclopedia of Natural Sciences	**503**
Natural Sciences	500
Encyclopedia	-03 (ss)
	= 500+03
Class No.	503

Periodicals of Decorative arts	**705**
Decorative arts	700
Periodicals	-05 (ss)
	= 700+05
Class No.	705

Philosophy and theory of Photography	**770.1**
Photography	770
Philosophy and theory	-01 (ss)
	= 770+01
Class No.	770.1

Use of standard subdivisions with one zero

If there is no indication of adding more than one zero, standard subdivisions may be used with one zero. Some examples of adding standard subdivisions with one zero are provided in the next few pages.

Philosophy of Library classification	**025.430 1**
Library classification	025.43
Philosophy	-01 (ss)
	= 025.43+01
Class No.	025.430 1
Classification of snakes	**597.960 12**
Snakes	597.96
Classification	-012 (ss)
	=597.96+012
Class No.	597.960 12
Terminology used in Inter Library Loan	**025.620 14**
Inter Library Loan	025.62
Terminology	-014 (ss)
	= 025.62+014
Class No.	025.620 14
Discourse and analysis ofVedanta philosophy	**181.480 141**
Vedanta philosophy	181.48
Discourse and analysis	-014 1 (ss)
	= 181.48+014 1
Class No.	181.480 141
Scientific principles of Labor economics	**331.015**
Labor economics	331
Scientific principles	-015 (ss)
	= 331+015

Class No.	331.015
Outline of Universal Decimal Classification	**025.432 020 2**
Universal Decimal Classification	025.432
Outline	-020 2 (ss)
	= 025.432+020 2
Class No.	025.432 020 2
Statistics in Taekwondo	**796.815 702 1**
Taekwondo	796.815 7
Statistics	-021 (ss)
	= 796.815 7+021
Class No.	796.815 702 1
Standards for general bibliographies in Japan	**017.02 18**
General bibliographies	017
Standards	-021 8 (ss)
Instruction	Add to base number -0218 notation 1-9 from Table 2
Japan	-52
	= 017+021 8+52
Class No.	017.021 852
Use of cartoons in elementary education	**372.022 2**
Elementary education	372
Cartoons	-022 2 (ss)
	= 372+022 2
Class No.	372.022 2

Cricket as a profession	**796.358 023**
Cricket	796.358
Subject as a profession	-023 (ss)
	= 796.358+023
Class No.	796.358 023

Astrology for mathematicians	**133.602 451**
Astrology	133.6
The Subject for persons in specific occupations	-024 (ss)
Instruction	Add to base number -024 notation 001-999
Mathematics	510
	=133.6+024+51
Class No.	133.602 451

(Note here zero from 510 has been removed because this is only to make the class number of three digits long)

Information technology for university libraries	**004.024 027 7**
Information technology	004
Subject for people in specific occupations	-024 (ss)
Instruction	Add to base number -024 notation 001-999
University Library	027.7
	= 004+024+027.7
Class No.	004.024 027 7

Directory of public libraries in Haryana	**027.402 554 558**

Public libraries	027.4
Directory	-025 (ss)
Instruction	Add to base number -025 notation 1-9 from Table 2
Haryana	-545 58
	= 027.4+025+545 58
Class No.	027.402 554 558

Trademarks for racing cars	**388.348 027 2**
Vehicles	388.34
Instruction	Add to base number 388.34 the numbers following 629.22 in 629.222-629.228
Racing cars	~~629.22~~8
Trademarks	-027 2 (ss)
	= 388.34+8+027 2
Class No.	388.348 027 2

Instruments for Leather Bookbinding	**686.342 028 4**
Leather Bookbinding	686.342
Instruments	-028 4(ss)
	= 686.342+028 4
Class No.	686.342 028 4

Computer Applications to libraries	**020.285**
Libraries	020
Computer Applications	-028 5 (ss)
	= 020+028 5
Class No.	020.285

Note: One zero is omitted as it was redundant.

Dictionary of evolutionary psychology	**155.703**
Evolutionary psychology	155.7
Dictionary	-03 (ss)
	= 155.7+03
Class No.	155.703

Encyclopedia of labor economics	**331.03**
Labor economics	331
Encyclopedia	-03 (ss)
	=331+03
Class No.	331.03

Journals on secondary education	**373.05**
Secondary education	373
Periodicals (Journals)	-05 (ss)
	=373+05
Class No.	373.05

Management of Political parties	**324.206 8**
Political parties	324.2
Management	-068 (ss)
	=324.2+068
Class No.	324.206 8

Personnel management of hotels	**647.940 683**

Hotels	647.94
Personnel management	-068 3 (ss)
	=647.94+068 3
Class No.	647.940 683

Marketing of reference and information services	**025.520 688**
Reference and Information services	025.52
Marketing	-068 8 (ss)
	=025.52+068 8
Class No.	025.520 688

Study programs on Astrology	**133.607**
Astrology	133.6
Study programs	-07 (ss)
	=133.6+07
Class No.	133.607

Apprenticeship in university libraries	**027.707 155**
University libraries	027.7
Apprenticeship	-071 55 (ss)
	=027.7+071 55
Class No.	027.707 155

Research methods in mathematical geography	**526.072 1**
Mathematical geography	526
Research methods	-072 1 (ss)

	=526+072 1
Class No.	526.072 1
Case studies on oil paintings	**751.450 723**
Oil paintings	751.45
Case studies	-072 3 (ss)
	=751.45+072 3
Class No.	751.450 723
Statistical methods in biochemistry	**572.072 7**
Biochemistry	572
Statistical methods	-072 7 (ss)
	=572+072 7
Class No.	572.072 7
Exhibition of theatrical scenery in Mumbai	**751.510 745 479 2**
Theatrical scenery	751.51
Exhibition	-074 (ss)
Instruction	Add to base number -074 notation 1-9 from Table 2
Mumbai	-547 92
	=751.51+074+547 92
Class No.	751.510 745 479 2
Awards for newspaper media in India	**070.172 079 54**
Television media	070.172
Awards	-079 (ss)
Instruction	Add to base number -079 notation 1-9 from Table 2

India	-54
	=070.172+079+54
Class No.	070.172 079 54
Gender role in Athletics	**796.081**
Athletics	796
Gender role	-081 (ss)
	=796+081
Class No.	796.081
Feminist Christian mythology	**230.082**
Christian mythology	230
Feminist (Women)	-082 (ss)
	=230+082
Class No.	230.082
Street music for adolescents	**781.532 083 5**
Street music	781.532
Adolescents	-083 5 (ss)
	=781.532+083 5
Class No.	781.532 083 5
Dressmaking in 19th century	**687.090 34**
Dressmaking	687
19th century	-090 34 (ss)
	=687+090 34
Class No.	687.090 34
Dewey Decimal Classification in 2010's	**025.431 090 512**

Dewey Decimal Classification	025.431
2010's	-090 512 (ss)
	=025.431+090 512
Class No.	025.431 090 512

Middle age Hindu mythology	**294.513 090 2**
Hinduism	294.5
Instruction	Add to base number 294.5 the numbers following 20 in 201-203
Mythology	201.3
Middle age	-090 2 (ss)
	=294.5+13+090 2
Class No.	294.513 090 2

Use of standard subdivisions with two zeros

Generally standard subdivisions are used with one zero. If the zero subdivisions of a number in a schedule are used for special purposes, use 001-009 for standard subdivisions At a number of places in the schedule the zero subdivisions have been used for other purposes. At such places instructions have also been provided to add standard subdivisions with two zeros. If the classifier has to add a standard subdivision to such a number where he/she is instructed to use double zero for ss, then he/she must use double zero. Some examples of using double zeros are illustrated in the next few pages.

Standards for Documentation	**025.002 18**
Documentation	025
Instruction	.001-.009 Standard subdivisions

Standards	-021 8 (ss)
	=025+002 18
Class No.	025.002 18
Libraries in 17th century	**027.009 031**
Libraries	027
Instruction	.001-.009
	Standard subdivisions
17th century	-090 31 (ss)
	=027+009 031
Class No.	027.009 031
Scientific principles of Eastern philosophy	**181.001 5**
Eastern philosophy	181
Instruction	.001-.007
	Standard subdivisions
Scientific Principles	-015 (ss)
	=184+001 5
Class No.	181.001 5
Encyclopedia of Christianity	**230.003**
Christianity	230
Instruction	.002-.003
	Standard subdivisions of Christianity
Encyclopedia	-03 (ss)
	=230+003
Class No.	230.003
Journals on kinds of states	**321.005**
Kinds of states	321

Instruction	.001-.009
	Standard subdivisions
Journals	-05 (ss)
	=321+005
Class No.	321.002 28

Classification of Political parties of Canada	**324.271 001 2**
Political parties of Canada	324.271
Instruction	.241 001-.241 009
	Standard subdivisions
Classification	-012 (ss)
	=324.271+001 2
Class No.	324.271 001 2

Research methods in Economic geography	**330.900 721**
Economic geography	330.9
Instruction	.900 1-.900 8
	Standard subdivisions
Research methods	-072 1 (ss)
	=330.9+007 21
Class No.	330.900 721

Dictionary of Personal finance	**332.024 003**
Personal finance	332.024
Instruction	.024 001-.024 007
	Standard subdivisions
Dictionary	-03 (ss)
	=332.024+003
Class No.	332.024 003

Teaching Public Finance in Brazil	**336.007 108 1**
Public Finance	336
Instruction	.007-.008
	Standard subdivisions
Teaching	-071 (ss)
Instruction	Add to base number -0710 notation 1-9 from Table 2
Brazil	81
	=336+007 10+81
Class No.	336.007 108 1

Correspondence courses in Private law	**346.007 15**
Private law	346
Instruction	.005-.008
	Standard subdivisions
	As modified under 342-347
Correspondence courses	-071 5 (ss)
	=346+071 5
Class No.	346.007 15

(Note the above instruction i.e. as modified under 342-347. And on reaching 342-347 it is found that ss 07 has not been modified.Hence you have to verify whether the ss has been modified or not before using the ss)

Use of maps in Military Science	**355.002 23**
Military Science	355
Instruction	.001-.009

	Standard subdivisions
Maps	-022 3 (ss)
	=355+002 23
Class No.	355.002 23
Computer applications to life Insurance	**368.320 028 5**
Life insurance	368.32
Instruction	Add to each subdivision identified by * as follows: .001-.005
	Standard subdivisions
Computer applications	-028 5 (ss)
	=368.32+002 85
Class No.	368.320 028 5
Adult education of young women	**374.008 422**
Adult education	374
Instruction	.003-.005
	Standard subdivisions
Young women	-084 22 (ss)
	=374+008 422
Class No.	374.008 422
Prehistoric algebra	**512.009 01**
Algebra	512
Instruction	.001-.009
	Standard subdivisions
Prehistoric	-090 1 (ss)
	=512+009 01
Class No.	512.009 01

Diagrams in Fluid mechanics	**532.002 23**
Fluid mechanics	532
Instruction	.001-.009
	Standard subdivisions
Diagrams	-022 3 (ss)
	=532+002 23
Class No.	532.002 3

Patents for Petrology	**552.002 72**
Petrology	552
Instruction	.001-.008
	Standard subdivisions
Patents	-027 2 (ss)
	=552+002 72
Class No.	552.002 72

Electronic journals on Disease	**616.005**
Disease	616
Instruction	.003-.006
	Standard subdivisions
Electronic journals	-05(ss)
	=616+005
Class No.	616.005

Continuing education in Surgery	**617.007 15**
Surgery	617
Instruction	.003-.007
	Standard subdivisions of Surgery
Continuing education	-071 5 (ss)

	=617+007 15
Class No.	617.007 15
Teaching of applied mechanics at college level	**620.100 711**
Applied mechanics	620.1
Instruction	.100 1-.100 9
	Standard subdivisions
Teaching at college level	- 071 1 (ss)
	=620.1+007 11
Class No.	620.100 711
Materials used in Animal husbandry	**636.002 84**
Animal husbandry	636
Instruction	.001-.009
	Standard subdivisions
Materials used in a subject	-028 4 (ss)
	=636+002 84
Class No.	636.002 84
Operations research in Textiles	**677.001 1**
Textiles	677
Instruction	.003-.009
	Standard subdivisions
Operations research	-011 (ss)
	=677+001 1
Class No.	677.001 1
Sacred music for retired people	**781.700 869 6**

Sacred music	781.7
Instruction	.700 1-.700 9
	Standard subdivisions
Retired people	-086 96 (ss)
	=781.7+008 696
Class No.	781.700 869 6

Encyclopedia of Chinese History	**951.003**
Chinese history	951
Instruction	Add as instructed under 930-990
Encyclopedia	-003
	=951+003
Class No.	951.003

(Note here that as per instructions under 930-990, to the numbers of history schedule from 930-990 the standard subdivisions are to be used with double zeros)

Use of standard subdivisions with three zeros

If the 00 subdivisions of a number in schedule also are used for special purposes, use 0001-0009 for standard subdivisions. Some examples have been provided below:

Directory of Special libraries	**026.000 25**
Special libraries	026
Instruction	.000 1-.000 5
	Standard subdivisions
Directory	-025 (ss)
	=026+000 25
Class No.	026.000 25

Encyclopedia of nonreligious subjects treated in Hadith	**297.125 180 003**

Nonreligious subjects treated in Hadith	297.125 18
Instruction	.125 180 001-.125 180 009
	Standard subdivisions
Encyclopedia	-03 (ss)
	=297.125 18+000 3
Class No.	297.125 180 003
Application of computer software to Service tax	**336.278 000 285 53**
Service tax	336.278
Instruction	.278 000 1-.278 000 9
	Standard subdivisions
Computer application	-028 5 (ss)
Instruction	Add to base number -0285 the numbers following 00 in 004-006
Software	005.3
	=336.278+000 285+53
Class No.	336.278 000 285 53
Models for Curricula	**375.000 228**
Curricula	375
Instruction	.000 1-.000 9
	Standard subdivisions
Models	-022 8 (ss)
	=375+000 228
Class No.	375.000 228
Statistics of demand for labor in industry and occupation	**331.123 100 021**

other than extractive, manufacturing, construction

Demand for labor......	331.123 1
Instruction	.123 100 01-.123 100 09
	Standard subdivisions
Statistics	-021 (ss)
	=331.132 1+000 21
Class No.	331.123 100 021

Print journals on Insurance law	**346.086 000 5**
Insurance law	346.086
Instruction	.086 000 1-.086 000 9
	Standard subdivisions
Print Journals	-05 (ss)
	=346.086+000 5
Class No.	346.086 000 5

Use of more than one standard subdivisions

In normal circumstances only one standard subdivision can be used. Do not add multiple standard subdivisions to the same number except when specifically instructed to do so, and in the following instances. 1. A standard subdivision may be added to standard subdivisions that have changed or extended meanings. For example, notation 03 from table 1, the standard subdivision for encyclopedias, may be added to 370.15 Educational psychology to represent encyclopedias of educational psychology 370.1503 because the regular meaning of 370.15 (scientific principles) has been discontinued to 370.1 and replaced by an extended meaning of the standard subdivision for psychological principles at this number. 2. When standard subdivisions are displaced to nonzero numbers (usually for geographic treatment), the full range of standard subdivisions may be added. For example: the management of penal institutions in Great Britain 365.941068.

However there is a provision of adding second standard subdivision with 04 Special Topics (standard subdivision). This standard subdivision can be added only when it is specially set forth in the schedules. The second standard subdivision from 01 to 09 can be added to it and its subdivisions as required. Some examples are illustrated below:

Participatory democracy in Afghanistan	**323.042 095 81**
Civil and political rights	323
Participatory democracy	.042 (ss)
2nd Standard subdivision	-09 (2nd ss)
Afghanistan	-581 (Table 2)
	=323+042+09+581
Class No.	323.042 095 81

Statistical graphs of Job creation in labor market	**331.120 424 021**
Labor market	331.12
Job creation	.042 4 (ss)
Statistical graphs (2nd Standard subdivision)	-021 (2nd ss)
	=331.12+042 4+021
Class No.	331.120 424 021

Encyclopedia of Solid-state Chemistry	**541.042 103**
Physical chemistry	541
Solid state chemistry	.042 1 (ss)

Encyclopedia (2nd Standard subdivision)	-03 (2nd ss)
	=541+042 1+03
Class No.	541.042 103

(Note .0421 (Solid-state Chemistry) is made by following instructions at .042)

Research on skyscrapers architecture	**720.483 072**
Architecture	720
Special topics	.4
Skyscrapers	.483 (ss)
Research (2nd Standard subdivision)	-072 (2nd ss)
	=720+483+072
Class No.	720.483 072

If any title requires application of more than one standard subdivision, then only one standard subdivision can be added. To decide which standard subdivision is to be added and which is to be avoided, the table of preference provided in volume 1 at the beginning of table 1 (page no. 180) must be followed. The table of preference is provided below for reference.

Special topics	-04
Biography	-092
Auxiliary techniques and procedure; apparatus, equipment, materials	-028
Education, research, related topics (Except -074, -075)	-07
Management	-068
Philosophy and theory	-01
The subject as a profession, occupation, hobby	-023

The subject for people in specific occupations	-024
Directories of persons and organizations	-025
Patents and identification marks	-027
Commercial miscellany	-029
Organizations	-0601-0609
Organizations (without subdivisions)	-06
Group of people	-08
Specific continents, countries, localities; extraterrestrial worlds	-093-099
Areas, regions, places in general	-091
Historical periods	-0901-0905
Museums, collections, exhibits	-074
Museum activities and services	-075
Illustrations, models, miniatures	-022
Tabulated and related materials	-021
Synopses and outlines	-0202
Humorous treatment	-0207
Audiovisual treatment	-0208
Dictionaries, encyclopedias, concordances	-03
History and geographic treatment (without subdivision)	-09
Serial publications	-05

Let us go through some examples:

Encyclopedia of Research on Psychology	**150.72**

Psychology	150
Encyclopedia	-03 (ss)
Research	-072 (ss)
	=150+072
Class No.	150.72

(Note here 07 has a preference over 03, as per table of preference and one zero of 150 has been removed as it is redundant)

Patents for Equipments in Chemical engineering	**660.028**
Chemical engineering	660
Patents	-021 8 (ss)
Equipments	-028 (ss)
	=660+028
Class No.	660.028

History of Teaching of Library science	**020.71**
Library science	020
Instruction	.001-.009
	Standard subdivisions
Teaching	-071 1 (ss)
History	-09 (ss)
	=020+071
Class No.	020.71

Journal on Personnel management of Central Banks	**332.110 683**
Central Banks	332.11
Personnel management	-068 3 (ss)
Journal	-05 (ss)

	=332.11+068 3
Class No.	332.110683
Study of Astrology in 13th Century	**133.607**
Astrology	133.6
Study	-07 (ss)
13th Century	-090 22 (ss)
	=133.6+07
Class No.	133.607
Humorous treatment of 14th Century tales about horses	**398.245 296 655 090 23**
Base Number	398.245 2
Instruction	Add to base number 398.245 2 the numbers following 59 in 592-599; then add further as instructed under 398.21-398.27
Horses	599.665 5
Humorous treatment	-020 7 (ss)
14th Century	-090 23 (ss)
	=398.245 2+966 55+090 23
Class No.	398.245 296 655 090 23

5

Use of Table 2: Areas

The Table 2 in DDC consists of notation for geographical locations. The numbers from Table 2 are never used alone, but may be used as required with any number from the schedules. These numbers can be added by three different ways viz. i. Direct use through instruction. ii. Through the standard subdivision -09, and iii. Through other tables. These ways are discussed with suitable examples in the next few pages.

ADDING AREAS WHEN THERE IS AN INSTRUCTION

At various places in the schedules, there are instructions regarding use of Table 2 i.e. Areas Table. In this case the area numbers are added directly from Table 2. For example in schedule of General libraries at the number 027.4 Public libraries there is such instruction under 027.43-.49. The instruction reads as under.

Add to base number 027.4 notation 3-9 from Table 2.

This is an add note which instruct the classifier to add the numbers 3 to 9 from Table 2 to the base number 027.4. Here the classifier only has to act step by step according to the instruction. For the convenience of the students these steps are illustrated below:

Suppose you have to classify a title "Public libraries in Haryana". You will find following add note at reaching the number 027.43-.49 in the schedule.

.4	Public libraries
.43-.49	Treatment by specific continents, countries, localities

Add to base number 027.4 notation 3-9 from Table 2.

You just follow the following steps and the class number is ready.

Step 1.	Note down the base number.	027.4
Step 2.	Go to Table 2 in volume 1 and search a number for Haryana between 3 to 9	-545 58
Step 3.	Suffix the number taken from Table 2 to the base number	027.554558

(As a matter of mnemonic and convenience a blank space is provided after each three letter starting from the sixth letter. Hence our class number will look like: 027.554 558)

This is the first way of adding areas notation from Table 2. You have already made the class numbers using Table 2 from Law, and Geography and History schedules. Let us try more examples of the same nature.

National Library of Canada	**027.571**
National Libraries	027.5
Instruction	Add to base number 027.5 notation 3-9 from Table 2
Canada (Table 2)	-71
	=027.5+71
Class No.	027.571

School Libraries in Uttarakhand	**027.854 51**
School Libraries	027.8
Instruction	Add to base number 027.8 notation 3-9 from Table 2
Uttarakhand (Table 2)	-545 1
	=027.8+545 1
Class No.	027.854 51
College Libraries in Puducherry	**027.754 86**
School Libraries	027.7
Instruction	Add to base number 027.7 notation 3-9 from Table 2
Puducherry (Table 2)	-548 6
	=027.7+548 6
Class No.	027.754 86
The Hindustan Times	**079.54**
Journalism and newspapers in other geographic areas	079
Instruction	Add to base number 079 notation 1-9 from Table 2
India (Table 2)	-54
	=079+54
Class No.	079.54
Migration of people from India to USA	**304.854 073**
Migration	304.8
Instruction	Add to base number 304.8 notation 3-9 from Table 2;

	then add 0 and to the result add notation 1-9 from Table 2
India (Table 2)	-54
Add 0	0
USA (Table 2)	-73
	=304.8+54+0+73
Class No.	304.854 073

Political conditions in Egypt	**320.962**
Political situation and conditions	320.9
Instruction	Add to base number 320.9 notation 01-9 from Table 2
Egypt (Table 2)	-62
	=320.9+62
Class No.	320.962

Voting behavior in Haiti	**324.972 94**
Voting behavior	324.9
Instruction	Add to base number 324.2 notation 4-9 from Table 2
Haiti (Table 2)	-729 4
	=324.9+729 4
Class No.	324.972 94

Communist party of India	**324.254 075**
Political parties	324.2
Instruction	Add to base number 324.2 notation 4-9 from Table 2 ; then add to the number according to the table below

India (Table 2)	-54
Communist parties	075
	=324.2+54+075
Class No.	324.254 075

Economic conditions of New Zealand	**330.993**
Economic situation and conditions	330.9
Instruction	Add to base number 330.9 notation 3-9 from Table 2
New Zealand (Table 2)	-93
	=330.9+93
Class No.	330.993

Military assistance to Pakistan	**355.032 549 1**
Military assistance	355.032
Instruction	Add to base number 355.032 notation -3-9 from Table 2
Pakistan (Table 2)	-549 1
	=355.032+549 1
Class No.	355.032 549 1

Primary education in Brazil	**372.981**
Primary education	372
Instruction	Add to base number 372.9 notation 1-9 from Table 2
Brazil (Table 2)	-81
	=372.9+81
Class No.	372.981

Geology of Caribbean Sea	**551.461 365**
Oceanography and marine geology	551.46
Instruction	Add to base number 551.461 the numbers following -16 in notation -163-167 from Table 2
Caribbean Sea Africa (Table 2)	~~-16~~3 65 =551.461+365
Class No.	551.461 365
Flora of Norway	**581.948 1**
Flora (Natural history of plants)	581.9
Instruction	Add to base number 581.9 notation 3-9 from Table 2
Norway (Table 2)	-481 =581.9+481
Class No.	581.948 1
Fauna of Uzbekistan	**591.958 7**
Fauna (Natural history of animals)	591.9
Instruction	Add to base number 591.9 notation 3-9 from Table 2
Uzbekistan (Table 2)	-587 =591.9+587
Class No.	591.958 7
Management of restaurants in Sweden	**647.954 85**
Restaurants	647.95
Instruction	Add to base number

	647.95 notation 3-9 from Table 2
Sweden (Table 2)	-485
	=647.95+485
Class No.	647.954 85

Hangings textiles in Algeria	**746.396 5**
Hangings textiles	746.39
Instruction	Add to base number 746.39 notation 1-9 from Table 2
Algeria (Table 2)	-65
	=746.39+65
Class No.	746.396 5

Hunting and shooting sports in Guiana	**799.298 8**
Hunting and shooting sports	799.29
Instruction	Add to base number 799.29 notation 1-9 from Table 2
Guiana (Table 2)	-88
	=799.29+88
Class No.	799.298 8

ADDING AREAS WHEN THERE IS NO INSTRUCTION

When there is no instruction regarding the use of area table in the schedule and there is a requirement of area number. In such a case the classifier can add the area number through the standard subdivision 09 History, geographic treatment, biography. There is a provision of adding areas table under standard subdivision 09. You will find instructions to this effect under -091, -092 2 and -093-099. The instructions read as under.

At -091	Add to base number -091 the numbers following -1 in notation 11-19 from table 2
At -092 2	Add to base number -092 2 notation 3-9 from table 2
At -093-099	Add to base number -09 notation 3-9 from table 2; then add further as follows

Therefore, we can use areas table through the standard subdivision -09. In case you will use areas table through -091 & -093-099, you can add the numbers directly from Table 2 to the -09. But while adding areas number though -092 2, you have to add areas numbers to -092 2. The most important thing here to remember is that while adding areas standard subdivision, you have to keep in mind the use of number of zeros. It depends on the instructions to this effect in the schedules. Let us try some examples.

Local-area-networks in Developing countries	**004.680 917 24**
Local-area- networks	004.68
History, geographic treatment, biography (SS)	-09
Developing countries (Table 2)	-172 4 =004.68+09+172 4
Class No.	004.680 917 24

Educational role of libraries in Gujarat	**021.2409 547 5**
Educational role	021.24
History, geographic treatment, biography (SS)	-09
Gujarat (Table 2)	-547 5

	=021.24+09+547 5
Class No.	021.240 954 75

Child psychology in Mississippi county	**155.409 767 95**
Child psychology	155.4
History, geographic treatment, biography (SS)	-09
Mississippi county (Table 2)	-767 95
	=155.4+09+767 95
Class No.	155.409 767 95

Ethics of friendship in Libya	**177.620 961 2**
Ethics of friendship	177.62
History, geographic treatment, biography (SS)	-09
Libya (Table 2)	-612
	=177.62+09+612
Class No.	177.620 961 2

Islam in Pakistan	**297.095 491**
Islam	297
History, geographic treatment, biography (SS)	-09
Pakistan (Table 2)	-549 1
	=297+09+549 1
Class No.	297.095 491

Trade unions in Haryana	**331.880 954 558**
Trade unions	331.88
History, geographic treatment, biography (SS)	-09

Haryana (Table 2)	-545 58
	=331.88+09+545 58
Class No.	331.880 954 558
Military resources in USA	**355.209 73**
Military resources	355.2
History, geographic treatment, biography (SS)	-09
USA (Table 2)	-73
	=355.2+09+73
Class No.	355.209 73
Services of nurses in Melbourne	**362.173 099 451**
Services of nurses	362.173
History, geographic treatment, biography (SS)	-09
Melbourne (Table 2)	-945 1
	=362.173+09+945 1
Class No.	362.173 099 451
Distance education in Manila	**374.509 599 16**
Distance education	374.5
History, geographic treatment, biography (Table 1)	-09
Manila (Table 2)	-599 16
	=374.5+09+599 16
Class No.	374.509 599 16
Geodetic surveying in Serbia	**526.309 497 1**

Geodetic surveying	526.3
History, geographic treatment, biography (Table 1)	-09
Serbia (Table 2)	-497 1
	=526.3+09+4971
Class No.	526.309 497 1
Corn crops in Bhutan	**633.150 954 98**
Corn crops	633.15
History, geographic treatment, biography (SS)	-09
Bhutan (Table 2)	-549 8
	=633.15+09+549 8
Class No.	633.150 954 98
Beets horticulture in Denmark	**635.110 948 9**
Beets horticulture	635.11
History, geographic treatment, biography (SS)	-09
Denmark (Table 2)	-489
	=635.11+09+489
Class No.	635.110 948 9
Technology for production of fertilizers in Wales	**668.620 942 9**
Fertilizers	668.62
History, geographic treatment, biography (SS)	-09
Wales (Table 2)	-429
	=668.62+09+429
Class No.	628.620 942 9

Interior Lighting in Hospital Library building in Tonga	**621.322 782 662 099 612**
Base Number	621.322
Instruction	Add to base number 621.322 the numbers following 72 in 725-728
Library building	~~72~~7.82
Instruction	Add to base number ~~72~~7.82 the numbers following 027 in 027.1-027.8
Hospitals Library	~~027~~.662
History, geographic treatment, biography (SS)	-09 (ss)
Tonga (Table 2)	-961 2
	= 621.322 + 782 + 662 + 09 + 961 2
Class No.	621.322 782 662 099 612

Control of Chewing lice in Spinach crops in Amazon region	**635.419 757 098 616**
Base Number (Spinach *)	635.41
Instruction	Except for modification shown under specific entries, add to each subdivision identified by * as follows:
Injuries, disease, pests	9
Instruction	Add to 9 the numbers following 632 in 632.1-632.9
Insect pests	~~632~~.7

Instruction	Add to base number 632.7 the numbers following 595.7 in 595.72-595.79
Chewing lice	595.757
History, geographic treatment, biography (SS)	-09 (ss)
Amazon region (Table 2)	-861 6
	=635.41+9+7+57+09+861 6
Class No.	635.419 757 098 616
Architecture of hotels building in Chennai	**728.509 548 2**
Base Number	728.5
History, geographic treatment, biography (Table 1)	-09 (ss)
Chennai (Table 2)	-548 2
	=728.5+09+548 2
Class No.	728.509 548 2
Control of air pollution in Hungary	**363.739 209 439**
Air pollution	363.739 2
Instruction	Except for modification shown under specific entries, add to each subdivision identified by * as follows:
Control	6
History, geographic treatment, biography (SS)	-09 (ss)

Hungary (Table 2)	-439
	=363.739 2+09+439
Class No.	363.739 209 439
Beriberi disease in Romania	**616.392 009 498**
Base Number (Beriberi *)	616.392
History, geographic treatment, biography (Table 1)	-09
Romania (Table 2)	-498
	=616.392+009+498
Class No.	616.392 009 498
Plastic surgery of nose in Turkey	**617.523 059 200 956 1**
Base Number (Nose *)	617.523
Instruction	Except for modification shown under specific entries, add to each subdivision identified by * as follows:
Plastic surgery	0592
History, geographic treatment, biography (Table 1)	-09
Turkey (Table 2)	-561
	=617.523+059 2+009+561
Class No.	617.523 059 200 956 1
Diagnosis of virus disease in goats in Central America	**636.390 896 910 600 972 8**
Base Number	636.390

Instruction	Add to base number 636.390 the numbers following 636.0 in 636.001-636.08
Veterinary medicine	~~636.0~~89
Instruction	Add to base number 636.089 the numbers following 61 in 610-618
Virus disease*	~~61~~6.91
Instruction	Except for modification shown under specific entries, add to each subdivision identified by * as follows:
Treatment	06
History, geographic treatment, biography (Table 1)	-09
Central America (Table 2)	-728
	= 636.390 + 89 + 691 + 06 + 009 + 728
Class No.	636.390 896 910 600 972 8

Special libraries in Mumbai	**026.000 954 792**
Special libraries	026
Instruction	.000 7-.000 9 Standard subdivisions
History, geographic treatment, biography (SS)	-09 (ss)
Mumbai (Table 2)	-547 92
	=026+000 9+547 92
Class No.	026.000 954 792

Service tax in Portugal	**336.278 000 946 9**
Service tax	336.278
Instruction	.278 000 1-.278 000 9
	Standard subdivisions
History, geographic treatment, biography (SS)	-09 (ss)
Portugal (Table 2)	-469
	=336.278+000 9+469
Class No.	336.278 000 946 9

ADDING AREAS TABLE THROUGH OTHER TABLES

Areas table can also be added through other tables like Table 1 and Table 5. You have already seen the use of areas table through standard subdivision -09. This provision is general and classifier can add area notation through -09 on his own as and when required so. In Table 1, there are other instances too where a provision of adding areas table is made.

Law as a profession in Netherlands	**340.234 92**
Law	340
Subject as a profession (Table 1)	-023
Instruction	Add to base number -023 notation 1-9 from Table 2
Netherlands (Table 2)	-492
	=340+23+492
Class No.	340.234 92

Patents on wheat in Ukraine	**633.110 272 477**
Wheat	633.11
Patents (Table 1)	-027 2

Instruction	Add to base number -027 2 notation 1-9 from Table 2
Ukraine (Table 2)	-477
	=633.11+027 2+477
Class No.	633.110 272 477

Commercial miscellany of milk processing in Poland	**637.102 943 8**
Milk processing	637.1
Commercial miscellany (Table 1)	-029
Instruction	Add to base number -029 notation 1-9 from Table 2
Poland (Table 2)	-438
	=637.1+029+438
Class No.	637.102 943 8

Research in Solid State Physics in Siberia	**530.410 720 57**
Solid State Physics	530.41
Research (Table 1)	-072
Instruction	Add to base number -072 0 notation 1-9 from Table 2
Siberia (Table 2)	-57
	=530.41+072 0+57
Class No.	530.410 720 57

Competitions of wrestling in Pakistan	**796.812 079 549 1**
Wrestling	796.812
Competitions (Table 1)	-079
Instruction	Add to base number -079

	notation 4-9 from Table 2
Pakistan (Table 2)	-549 1
	=796.812+079+549 1
Class No.	796.812 079 549 1

The above are the instances of adding area table through table 1. Now we will look how area table can be added through Table 5. In Table 5, there is an instruction in the beginning to add areas table to any number in Table 5. Let us try a couple of examples.

Social status of Paharis in Canada	**305.891 496 071**
Social status of Ethnic and national groups	305.8
Instruction	Add to base number 305.8 notation 1-9 from Table 5
Paharis (Table 5)	-914 96
Instruction	Except where instructed otherwise, and unless it is redundant, add 0 to the number from this table and to the result add notation 1 or 3-9 from Table 2
Canada (Table 2)	-71
	=305.8+914 96+0+71
Class No.	305.891 496 071

Civil rights of Romanians in China	**323.115 910 51**
Base number	323.11
Instruction	Add to base number 323.11 notation 1-9 from Table 5

Romanians (Table 5)	-591
Instruction	Except where instructed otherwise, and unless it is redundant, add 0 to the number from this table and to the result add notation 1 or 3-9 from Table 2 in China
China (Table 2)	-51
	=323.11+591+0+51
Class No.	323.115 910 51
Art of Bulgarians in Tunisia	**704.039 181 106 11**
Base number	704.03
Instruction	Add to base number 704.03 notation 05-9 from Table 5
Bulgarians (Table 5)	-918 11
Instruction	Except where instructed otherwise, and unless it is redundant, add 0 to the number from this table and to the result add notation 1 or 3-9 from Table 2
Tunisia (Table 2)	-611
	=704.03+918 11+0+611
Class No.	704.039 181 106 11
Ethno psychology of Nepalis in West Bengal	**155.849 149 505 414**
Base number	155.84
Instruction	Add to base number 155.84 notation 1-9 from

	Table 5
Nepalis (Table 5)	-914 95
Instruction	Except where instructed otherwise, and unless it is redundant, add 0 to the number from this table and to the result add notation 1 or 3-9 from Table 2
West Bengal (Table 2)	-541 4
	=155.84+914 95+0+541 4
Class No.	155.849 149 505 414

USE OF TWO NUMBERS FROM TABLE 2

There is a provision of adding two numbers from Table 2 to a number from schedules. One such option is provided under area table itself under -1 Areas, regions, places in general. Here the instruction reads as follows:

(Option: Add to each number in -1 as follows:

03-09 Treatment by continent, country, locality

Add to 0 notation 3-9 from Table 2

In this way we have an option to add two numbers from Table 2 to any number from the schedules. For example:

Private libraries in rural areas of Punjab	**027.117 340 545 52**
Private libraries	027.1
Instruction	Add to base number 027.4 notation 1-9 from Table 2
Rural areas (Table 2)	-173 4
Connecting digit	0
Punjab (Table 2)	-545 52
	=027.1+173 4+0+545 58

Class No.	027.117 340 545 52
Adult education in Western blocs of Oakland	**374.917 130 794 66**
Adult education	374.9
Instruction	Add to base number 374.9 notation 1-9 from Table 2
Western blocs (Table 2)	-171 3
Connecting digit	0
Oakland (Table 2)	-794 66
	=374.9+171 3+0+794 66
Class No.	374.917 130 794 66
Maps of deserts of Libya	**912.191 540 612**
Maps	912.19
Instruction	Add to base number 912.19 the numbers following -1 in notation -11-19 from Table 2
Deserts (Table 2)	-154
Connecting digit	0
Libya (Table 2)	-612
	=912.19+154+0+612
Class No.	912.191 540 612

In addition to this there are instructions at some places in the schedules to add two numbers from Table 2 and the connecting digit is 0. For example:

Foreign relations between Hungary and Norway	**327.439 048 1**
Foreign relations	327
Instruction	Add to base number 327 notation 3-9 from Table 2;

	then, for relations between that nation or region and another nation or region, add 0 and to the result add notation 1-9 from Table 2
Hungary (Table 2)	-439
Connecting digit	0
Norway (Table 2)	-481
	=327+439+0+481
Class No.	327.439 041 8

Foreign economic relations between Greece and Canada	**337.495 071**
Foreign economic relations	337
Instruction	Add to base number 337 notation 01-9 from Table 2; then, for relations between that nation or region and another nation or region, add 0 and to the result add notation 1-9 from Table 2
Greece (Table 2)	-495
Connecting digit	0
Canada (Table 2)	-71
	=337+495+0+71
Class No.	337.495 071

Cultural exchange between USA and India	**303.482 730 54**
Cultural exchange	303.482
Instruction	Add to base number 303.482 notation 1-9 from

	Table 2; then add 0 and then again add notation 1-9 from Table 2
USA (Table 2)	-73
Connecting digit	0
India (Table 2)	-54
	=303.482+73+0+54
Class No.	337.482 730 54

Migration from Punjab to Canada	**304.871 054 552**
Migration	304.8
Instruction	Add to base number 304.8 notation 3-9 from Table 2; then add 0 and to the result add notation 1-9 from Table 2 for the place of origin
Canada (Table 2)	-71
Connecting digit	0
Punjab (Table 2)	-545 52
	=304.8+71+0+545 52
Class No.	304.871 054 552

Chinese educational aid to Iran	**379.129 550 51**
Educational aid	379.129
Instruction	Add to base number 379.129 notation 1-9 from Table 2; then for area providing support, add 0 and again add notation 1-9 from Table 2

Iran (Table 2)	-55
Connecting digit	0
China (Table 2)	-51
	=379.129+55+0+51
Class No.	379.129 550 5 1

6

Use of Table 3: Subdivisions for the Arts, for Individual Literatures, for Specific Literary Forms

The Table 3 in DDC consists of notations for the arts, for individual literatures, and for specific literary forms. Like other tables in DDC this table is also never used alone, but may be used as required by add notes under subdivisions of individual literatures or with base numbers for individual literatures identified by * under 810-890. It is clearly mentioned in the beginning of the table that the notation from this table can be used only with subdivisions of individual literature, which are identified with *. Hence you have to make it sure that the subdivision of individual literature to which you are adding notation from Table 3 must have been identified by *. The subdivisions of individual literature which are not identified with * ends with language notation. Notation from Table 3 may also be used where instructed in 700.4, 791.4, 808-809.

The Table 3 is further divided into three sub-tables viz.:

1. Table 3A for description, critical appraisal, biography, single or collected works of an individual author.
2. Table 3B for description, critical appraisal, biography, single or collected works of two or more authors; also for rhetoric in specific literary forms.
3. Table 3C for additional elements used in number building within Table 3B and as instructed in 704, 791.4, 808-809.

The class numbers of literature is made from different elements viz. Base number; form; period; kind; scope, or medium; notation 08 collections or notation 09 criticism; sub-form; additional notation from Table 3C and other tables. Any literary work could be of one of two types i.e. either it is written by single author or by two or more authors. Both these categories have their different procedures for number building. Let us understand these procedures in the form of flow chart (*given on next pages*).

The procedure explained in the flow chart form is described at the beginning of Table 3A and 3B. This procedure is explained hereunder as step-by-step procedure. In this procedure the classifier has to take a decision at every crossing. The procedure provided under Table 3A is as under:

1. Look in the schedule 810-890 to find the base number for the language. The base number may be identified in an add note, e.g. at 851-858 ("add to base number 85") or another note, e.g., at 897 ("897.19 Aleut"); otherwise, it is the number given for the literature, e.g. Urdu-language literature 891.439. If there is a

FLOW CHART FOR WORKS BY OR ABOUT AN INDIVIDUAL AUTHOR

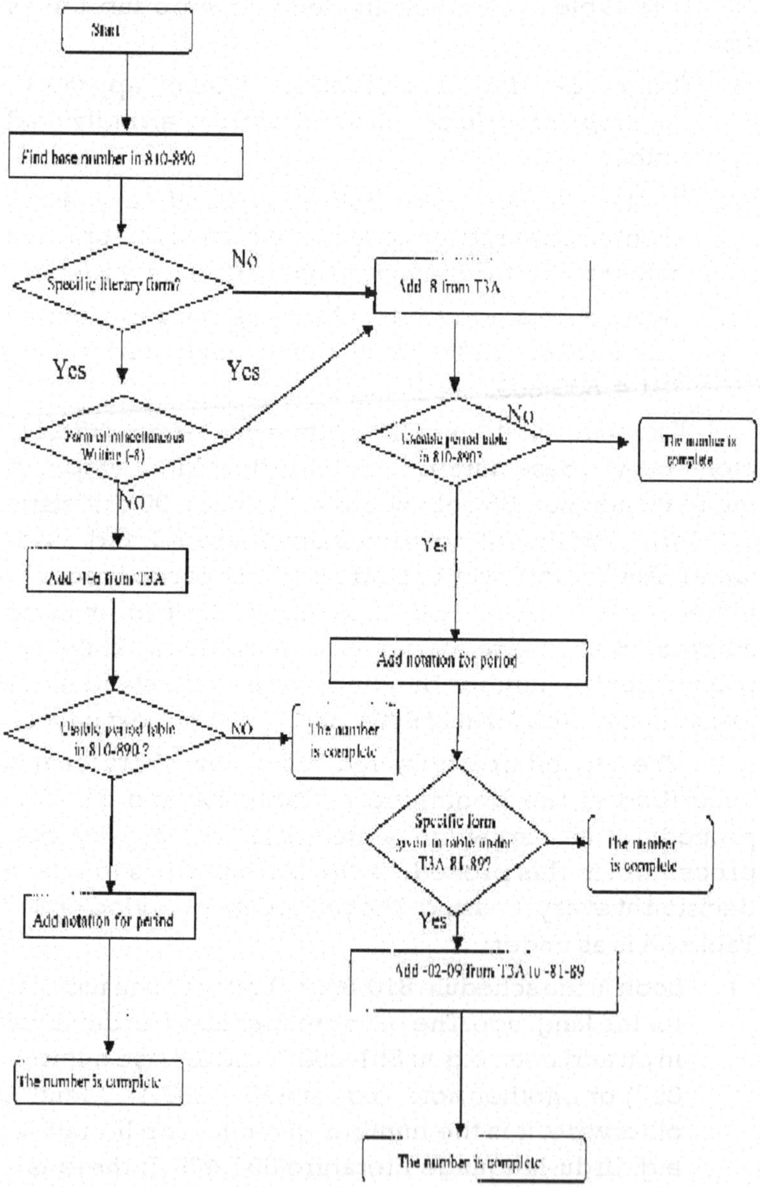

FLOW CHART FOR WORKS BY OR ABOUT MORE THAN ONE AUTHOR

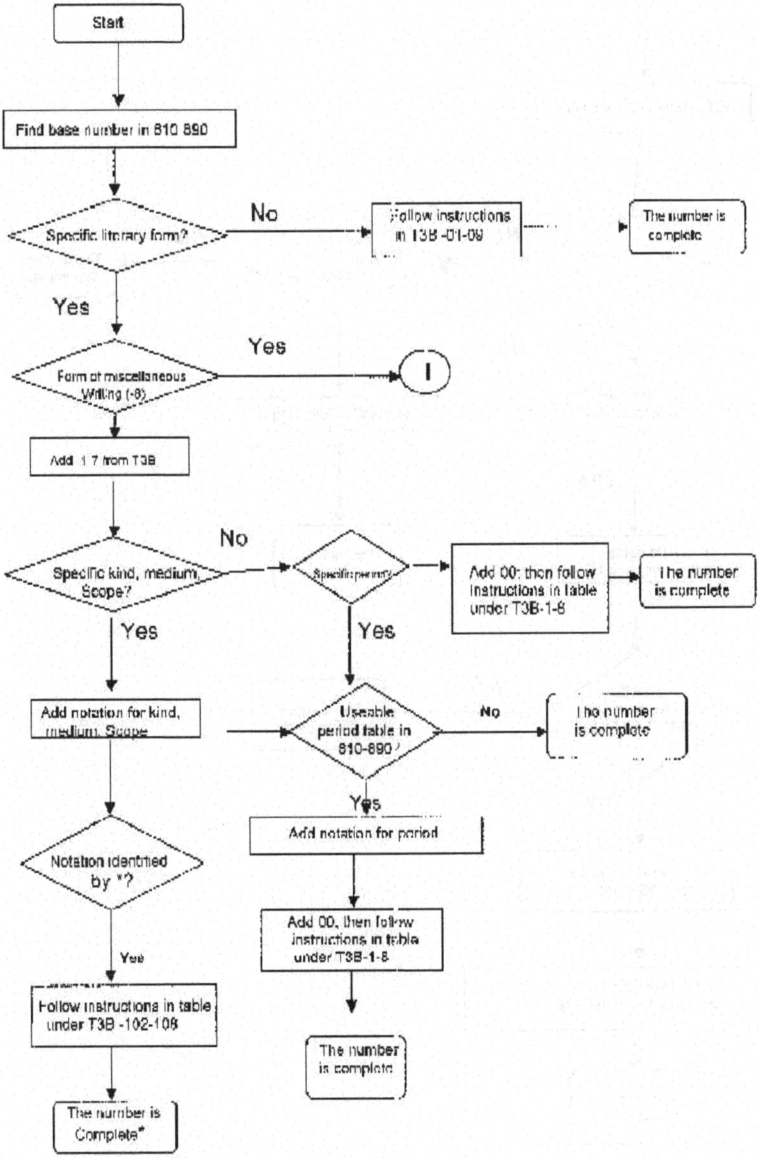

* If appropriate, standard subdivisions may be added

FLOW CHART FOR NOTATION 8 MISCELLANEOUS WRITINGS

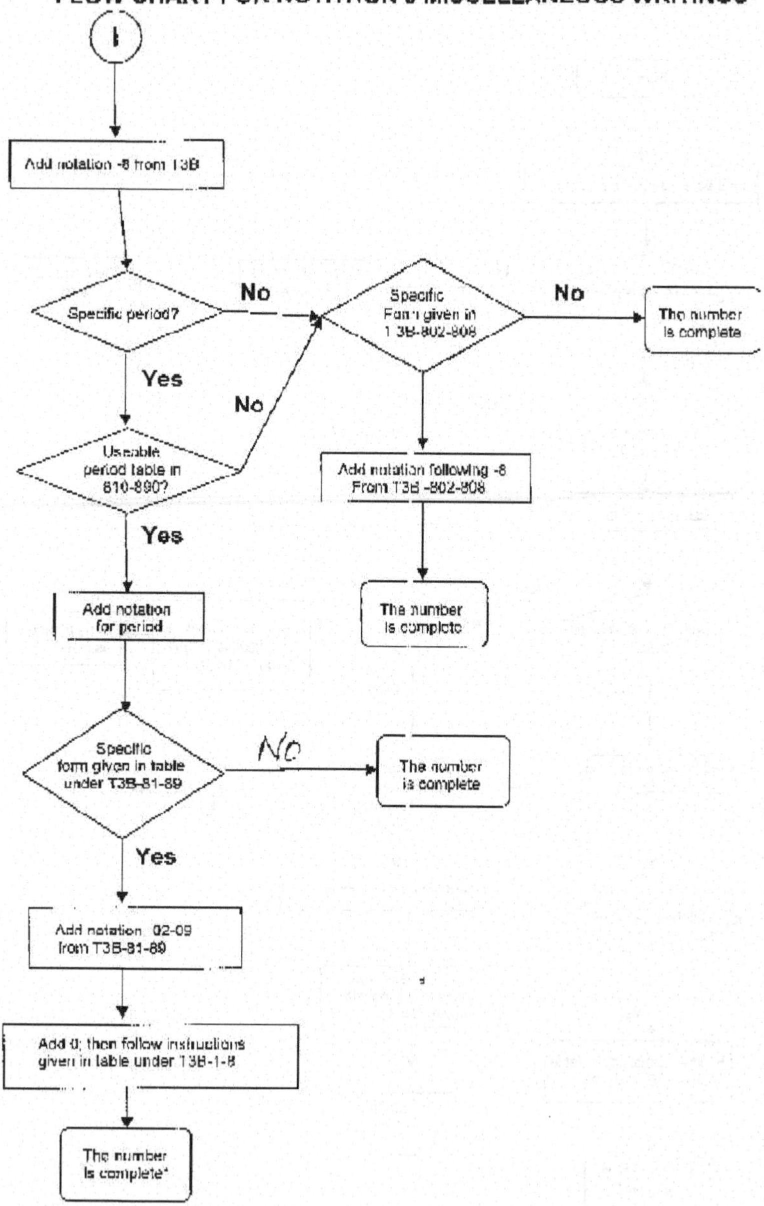

* If appropriate, standard subdivisions may be added

specific literary form, go to step 2; if not, go to the instructions under -8 in Table 3A.

2. In Table 3A find the correct subdivision for the literary form, e.g. Drama-2. Add this to base number, e.g. Urdu Drama 891.439 2, Aleut Drama 897.192. If the literary form appears as a subdivision of -8 miscellaneous writings, go to the instructions under-8 in Table 3A; otherwise go to step 3.
3. Turn back to the appropriate number in the schedule 810-890 to see whether there is an applicable period table. If there is one, go to step 4; if not, complete the class number by inserting a point between third and fourth digits, e.g. Nepali Drama by a 20th Century author 891.495 2.
4. Select the appropriate period number. Add this number to the number already derived; always insert a point after the third digit. The class number is complete (except for William Shakespeare), since standard subdivisions are never added for individual authors, e.g. Spenser's Faerie Queen 821.3 (821 English Poetry + 3 Elizabethan period).

The procedure provided under Table 3B is as under:

1. Look in the schedule 810-890 to find the base number for the language. The base number may be identified in an add note, e.g. at 851-858 ("add to base number 85") or another note, e.g., at 897 ("897.19 Aleut"); otherwise, it is the number given for the literature, e.g. Urdu-language literature 891.439. If there is a specific literary form, go to step 2; if not, go to step 8.
2. In Table 3B find the subdivision for the literary form, e.g. Drama. Add this to the base number e.g. English Drama 822, Dutch poetry 839.311. If the literary form appears as a subdivision of -8 Miscellaneous writings, go to the instructions under -8 in Table 3B. If

the work deals with poetry, drama, fiction, or speech of specific media, scopes, kinds for which there is special notation in Table 3B (e.g., -2041 One-act plays), go to step 3. For other works that deals with or fall within a limited time span, go to step 4. A limited time span is (1) fewer than three literary periods or (2) a single century. For other works not limited by time period, go to step 7.

3. Use the notation in Table 3B for the kind of poetry, drama, fiction, or speech, e.g. One-act plays in English literature 822.041. Insert a point after the third digit. Check whether the specific form is (1) the sole kind in a heading identified by * or (2) is named in a subdivisions-are-added note as a kind for which subdivisions may be added or (3) appears in a class-here note under a heading identified by *. If none of these conditions holds, the number is complete, e.g. collections of tragedies in English 822.0512. If one of the three conditions does hold, follow the instructions in the table under -102-107 in Table 3B. Following these instructions will involve using Table 3C for literature of specific periods, literature displaying specific features or emphasizing specific subjects, and literature for and by specific kinds of persons, e.g., collections of English sonnets 821.042 08, collections of English sonnets about love 821.042 083 543.

4. Turn back to the appropriate number in the schedule 810-890 to see whether there is an applicable period table. If there is one, go to step 4; if not, complete the class number by inserting a point between third and fourth digits, e.g. Nepali Drama by a 20th Century author 891.495 2.

5. Select the appropriate period number. Add this number to the number already derived, e.g. English

poetry of Elizabethan period 821.3; always insert a point after the third digit. Go to step 6.

6. Under the number for the literary form in Table 3B, go to the subdivisions for specific periods, e.g., under -2 for Drama go to -21-29. Follow the instructions given there, which will lead to adding the numbers following -10 in notation 1001-1009 of this table. For literature displaying specific features, literature emphasizing subjects, and literature for and by groups of people, the instructions at-1001-1009 will lead to use of Table 3C, e.g., critical appraisal of idealism in English Elizabethan drama 822.30913.
7. If the work is not limited by time period, go to the first subdivisions under the particular form in Table 3B, e.g., under -2 for drama go to -2001-2009. Follow the instructions given there, to add the numbers following -10 in notation -1001-1009 of this table. For literature displaying specific features, literature emphasizing subjects, and literature for and by specific groups of people, the instructions at -1001-1009 will lead to use of Table 3C, e.g., collections of English poetry by rural authors 821.008091734.
8. If the work is not limited to a specific literary form, consult -01-09 in Table 3B. Follow the instructions at the number selected, making use of Table 3C when specified, e.g., collections of English literature in many forms about holidays 820.80334. Use period notation 08001-08009 and -09001-09009 only if there is an applicable period table.

The procedure is well explained with examples and it can be easily followed. The examples of use of Table 3A, 3B, and 3C are provided in the following pages.

American poetry in English by a 20th century author	**821.5**
Base number	82
Poetry (Table 3A)	-1
Twentieth century (Table under 811-818)	5 =82+1+5
Class No.	821.5

German drama by a nineteenth century author	**832.7**
Base number	83
Drama (Table 3A)	-2
Nineteenth century (Table under 831-838)	7 =83+2+7
Class No.	832.7

French fiction by a renaissance period author	**843.3**
Base number	84
Fiction (Table 3A)	-3
Renaissance period (Table under 841-848)	3 =84+3+3
Class No.	843.3

Catalan essays by a 21st century author	**849.946**
Base number	849.9
Essays (Table 3A)	-4
21st Century (Table under 849.9)	6
	=849.9+4+6
Class No.	849.946

Italian speeches by a 16th century author	**855.4**
Base number	85
Speeches (Table 3A)	-5
16th century (Table under 850.1-858)	4 =85+5+4
Class No.	855.4
Collections of Punjabi romantic fictions	**891.423 085 08**
Base number	891.42
Romantic fictions (Table 3B)	-308 5
Instruction	* add as instructed under -102-107
Collections (Table 3B)	-08
	=891.42+308 5+08
Class No.	891.423 085 08
Collections of postmodernism Hindi Poetry	**891.431 008 011**
Base number	891.43
Poetry (Table 3B)	-1
Collections displaying specific features	-100 801-100 809
Instruction	Add to 100 80 notation 1-9 from Table 3C
Postmodernism (Table 3C)	-11
	=891.43+100 80+11
Class No.	891.431 008 011
Kolkata as depicted in Bengali Poetry	**891.441 008 032 541 47**

Base number	891.44
Poetry (Table 3B)	-1
Collections displaying specific features	100 801-100 809
Instruction	Add to 100 80 notation 1-9 from Table 3C
Places (Table 3C)	-32
Instruction	Add to -32 notation 1-9 from Table 2
Kolkata (Table 2)	-541 47
	= 891.44 + 100 + 80 + 32 + 541 47
Class No.	891.441 008 032 541 47

Collections of French drama on tigers	**842.008 036 297 56**
Base number	84
Drama (Table 3B)	-2
Instruction	Add to -200 the numbers following -100 in notation -1001-1009 of this table
Collections displaying specific features	100 801-100 809
Instruction	Add to ~~100~~ 80 notation 1-9 from Table 3C
Animals (Table 3C)	-362
Instruction	Add to -362 the

	numbers following 59 in 592-599
Tigers	~~59~~9.756
	= 84 + 200 +80 + 362 + 975 6
Class No.	842.008 036 297 56
Collected Biography of Korean poets	**895.710 09**
Base number	895.7
Poetry (Table 3B)	-1
History, description, critical appraisal Class here collected biography	-100 9 =895.7+100+9
Class No.	895.710 09
Collections of Old Persian novels by urban authors	**891.513 008 091 732**
Base number	891.51
Novels (Table 3B)	-3
Instruction	Add to -300 the numbers following -100 in notation -1001-1009 of this table
Collections ... by groups of people	~~100~~ 801-~~100~~ 809
Instruction	Add to -~~100~~ 80 notation 1-9 from Table 3C
Literature for and by persons resident (Table 3C) in specific regions	- 91
Instruction	Add to -91 the

	numbers following -1 in notation -11-19 from Table 2
Urban (Table 2)	-173 2
	= 891.51 + 300 + 80 + 91 + 173 2
Class No.	891.513 008 091 732

Collections of Oriya literature displaying temples	**891.456 080 382 035**
Base number	891.456
Collections of literary text (Table 3B)	-08
Instruction	Add to -080 notation 1-9 from Table 3C
Religious themes (Table 3C)	-382
Instruction	Add to base number -382 the numbers following 2 in 201-290
Temple	203.5
	= 891.456 + 080 + 382 + 035
Class No.	891.456 080 382 035

Collections of Urdu literature produced by Arabs	**891.439 080 892 7**
Base number	891.439
Collections of literary text (Table 3B)	-08
Instruction	Add to -080 notation 1-9 from Table 3C

Literature for and by persons of (Table 3C) ethnic and national groups	- 8
Instruction	Add to -8 notation 05-99 from Table 5
Arabs (Table 5)	-927
	= 891.439 + 080 + 8 + 927
Class No.	891.439 080 892 7

The collections of literary texts from more than two literatures are to be classified under 808. A few examples are as under:-

Collections of sonnets	**808.814 2**
Base number	808.81
Instruction	Add to base number 808.81 the numbers following -10 in notation 102-107 from Table 3B
Sonnets (Table 3B)	-~~10~~4 2
	=808.81+42
Class No.	808.814 2

Collections of poetry on everyday life	**808.819 355**
Base number	808.819
Instruction	Add to base number 808.819 notation 1-3 from Table 3C
Everyday life (Table 3C)	-355
	=808.819+355

Class No.	808.819 355
Collections of tragicomedy	**808.825 23**
Base number	808.82
Instruction	Add to base number 808.82 the numbers following -20 in 202-205 from Table 3B
Tragicomedy (Table 3B)	-~~20~~5 23
	=808.82+523
Class No.	808.825 23
Collections of short stories on folklore	**808.831 355 9**
Base number	808.83
Instruction	Add to base number 808.83 the numbers following -30 in 301-308 from Table 3B
Short stories* (Table 3B)	-~~30~~1
Instruction at -102-107	Add to 08 notation 1-9 from Table 3C
Folklore (Table 3C)	-355 9
	=808.83+1+3559
Class No.	808.831 355 9
Collections of narrative essays	**808.849 23**
Base number	808.849
Instruction	Add to base number 808.849 notation 1-3 from Table 3C
Narrative (Table 3C)	-23

	=808.849+23
Class No.	808.849 23
Collections of debates	**808.853**
Base number	808.85
Instruction	Add to base number 808.85 the numbers following -50 in 501-506 from Table 3B
Debates (Table 3B)	-503
	=808.85+3
Class No.	808.853
Collections of letters displaying love	**808.869 354 3**
Base number	808.869
Instruction	Add to base number 808.869 notation 1-3 from Table 3C
Love (Table 3C)	-354 3
	=808.869+353
Class No.	808.869 354 3
Collections of literary humor by Indians	**808.879 891 411**
Base number	808.879 8
Instruction	Add to base number 808.879 8 notation 1-9 from Table 5
Indians (Table 5)	-914 11
	=808.879 8+914 11
Class No.	808.879 891 411

7

Use of Table 4: Subdivisions of Individual Languages and Language Families

In DDC the Table 4 consists of notations for subdivisions of individual languages and language families. Like other tables in DDC this table is also never used alone, but may be used as required by add notes under subdivisions of specific languages and language families, or with the base numbers for individual languages identified by * as explained under 420-490. Notation from Table 1 can be added to the notation in Table 4 when appropriate. The classifier should be sure before using Table that the notation for the language either should be identified by * or there must be some add note with regard to use of Table 4. Examples of use of Table 4 are provided in next few pages.

A book on English phonology 421.5

Base number	42
Phonology (Table 4)	-15
	=42+15
Class No.	421.5
Use of adverbs in German language	**435.76**
Base number	43
Adverbs (Table 4)	-576
	=43+576
Class No.	435.76
Punctuation in Bengali language	**491.448 23**
Base number	491.44
Punctuation (Table 4)	-823
	=491.44+823
Class No.	491.448 23
Word formation in Danish language	**439.815 92**
Base number	439.81
Word formation (Table 4)	-592
	=439.81+592
Class No.	439.815 92
Remedial reading of Russian language	**491.784 2**
Base number	491.7
Instruction	Add to base number 491.78 the numbers following -8 in notation

	81-86 from Table 4
Remedial reading (Table 4)	-842
	=491.78+42
Class No.	491.784 2
Spelling and pronunciation of Hebrew language	**492.481 3**
Base number	492.4
Spelling and pronunciation (Table 4)	-813
	=492.4+813
Class No.	492.481 3
Generative grammar of Swedish language	**439.750 182**
Base number	439.7
Generative grammar (Table 4)	-501 82
	=439.7+501 82
Class No.	439.750 182
English Grammar	**425**
Base number	42
Grammar (Table 4)	-5
	=42+5
Class No.	425
Dictionary of Oriya idioms	**491.456 313**
Base number	491.456
Dictionary of idioms (Table 4)	-313
	=491.456+313
Class No.	491.456 313
Picture Dictionary of Czech language	**491.863 17**

Base number	491.86
Picture Dictionary (Table 4)	-317
	=491.86+317
Class No.	491.863 17
Dictionary of acronyms in Chinese language	**495.131 5**
Base number	495.1
Dictionary of acronyms (Table 4)	-315 =495.1+315
Class No.	495.131 5
Dictionary of homonyms in Panjabi language	**491.423 1**
Base number	491.42
Dictionary of homonyms (Table 4)	-31 =491.42+31
Class No.	491.423 1
Meaning of words in Maltese language	**492.798 1**
Base number	492.79
Meaning of words (Table 4)	-81
	=492.79+81
Class No.	492.798 1
Foreign elements in German language	**432.4**
Base number	43
Foreign elements (Table 4)	-24
	=43+24
Class No.	432.4

Sanskrit words in Telugu language	**494.827 249 12**
Base number	494
Instruction	Add to base number 494 the numbers following -94 in notation 941-948 from Table 6; then to the number for each language add further as instructed at beginning of Table 4
Telugu (Table 6)	-948 27
Foreign elements (Table 4)	-24
Instruction	Add to -24 notation 1-9 from Table 6
Sanskrit language (Table 6)	-912
	=494.827+24+912
Class No.	494.827 249 12

English words in Marathi language	**491.462 421**
Base number	491.46
Instruction	Add to base number 491.46 notation 1-8 from Table 4
Foreign elements (Table 4)	-24
Instruction	Add to -24 notation 1-9 from Table 6
English language (Table 6)	-21
	=491.46+24+21
Class No.	491.462 421

Alphabets in Bengali language 491.441 1

Base number	491.44
Alphabets (Table 4)	-11
	=491.44+11
Class No.	491.441 1

Use of German words in French language	**442.431**
Base number	44
Foreign elements (Table 4)	-24
Instruction	Add to -24 notation 1-9 from Table 6
German language (Table 6)	-31
	=44+24+31
Class No.	442.431

Translating from Sanskrit into Hindi language	**491.438 029 143 1**
Base number	491.43
Translating to and from other language (Table 4)	-802
Instruction	Add to -802 notation 2-9 from Table 6 for the language being translated from
Sanskrit language (Table 6)	-914 31
	=491.42+802+914 31
Class No.	491.428 029 143 1

Translating from Latin into Urdu language	**491.439 802 71**
Base number	491.439
Translating to and from other language (Table 4)	-802

Instruction	Add to -802 notation 2-9 from Table 6 for the language being translated from
Latin language (Table 6)	-71
	=491.439+802+71
Class No.	491.439 802 71

Structural approach to expression of Hindi for Russian speaking people **491.438 249 171**

Base number	491.43
Structural approach to expression for Persons whose native language is different (Table 4)	-824
Instruction	Add to -824 notation 2-9 from Table 6
Russian language (Table 6)	-917 1
	=491.43+824+917 1
Class No.	491.438 249 171

Structural approach to expression of Nepali for Tamil speaking people **491.495 824 948 11**

Base number	491.495
Structural approach to expression for Persons whose native language is different (Table 4)	-824
Instruction	Add to -824 notation 2-9 from Table 6
Tamil language (Table 6)	-948 11

	=491.495+824+948 11
Class No.	491.495 824 948 11
Audio-lingual approach to expression of Tajik language for Sindhi speaking people	**491.578 349 141 1**
Base number	491.57
Audio-lingual approach to expression for Persons whose native language is different (Table 4)	-834
Instruction	Add to -834 notation 2-9 from Table 6
Sindhi language (Table 6)	-914 11
	=491.57+834+914 11
Class No.	491.578 349 141 1
Audio-lingual approach to expression of Spanish for Khmer speaking people	**468.349 593 2**
Base number	46
Audio-lingual approach to expression for Persons whose native language is different (Table 4)	-834
Instruction	Add to -834 notation 2-9 from Table 6
Khmer language (Table 6)	-959 32
	=46+834+959 32
Class No.	468.349 593 2
English-language DDC classification Reader for	**428.640 240 254 31**

persons whose native language is not English	
Base number	42
Readers for persons in specific occupations (Table 4)	-864 024
Instruction	Add to -864024 notation 001-999
DDC classification (from schedule)	025.431 =42+864 024+025 431
Class No.	428.640 240 254 31
Hindi-language Artificial intelligence Reader for persons whose native language is not Hindi	**491.438 640 240 063**
Base number	491.43
Readers for persons in specific occupations (Table 4)	-864 024
Instruction	Add to -864024 notation 001-999
Artificial intelligence (from schedule)	006.3 =491.43+864 024+006.3
Class No.	491.438 640 240 063
German-language primer for peoples whose native language is Hindi	**438.649 143**
Base number	43
Readers for specific native language speakers (Table 4)	-864
Instruction	Add to -864 notation 2-9 from Table 6

Hindi language (Table 6)	-914 3 =43+864+914 31
Class No.	438.649 143 1
Chinese-language primer for peoples whose native language is Tamil	**495.186 494 811**
Base number	495.1
Readers for specific native language speakers (Table 4)	-864
Instruction	Add to -864 notation 2-9 from Table 6
Tamil language (Table 6)	-948 11 =495.1+864+948 11
Class No.	495.186 494 811
Rajasthani-language primer of cricket for peoples whose native language is English	**491.497 864 210 247 963 58**
Base number	491.497
Readers for specific native language speakers (Table 4)	-864
Instruction	Add to -864 notation 2-9 from Table 6; then add further as follows
English language (Table 6)	-21
Readers for persons in specific occupations	024
Instruction	Add to base number 024 notation 001-999
Cricket (from Schedule)	796.358 = 491.497 + 864 + 21 + 024 + 796.358

Class No.	491.497 864 210 247 963 58

Portuguese-language primer on Income Tax law for peoples whose native language is Hindi	**469.864 914 302 434 305 2**
Base number	469
Readers for specific native language speakers (Table 4)	-864
Instruction	Add to -864 notation 2-9 from Table 6; then add further as follows
Hindi language (Table 6)	-914 3
Readers for persons in specific occupations	024
Instruction	Add to base number 024 notation 001-999
Income Tax (from Schedule)	343.052
	=469+864+914 3 + 024 + 343.052
Class No.	469.864 914 302 434 305 2

Chinese systems of signing and fingerspelling of English	**428.915 1**
Base number	42
Specific systems of manual coding (Table 4)	-891
Instruction	Add to -891 notation 4-9 from Table 2
China (Table 2)	-51
	=42+891+51

Class No. 428.915 1

Bilingual dictionaries : A bilingual dictionary is one that gives words in one language and its meaning in a different language. As there are two languages involved, hence notation for both languages should be used. Now the question arises, which language should come first and which later. There is a specific provision for this problem in DDC. The provision is as under:-

1. A bilingual dictionary with entry words in only one language is classed with that language.
2. A bilingual dictionary with entry words in both languages aimed at speakers of only one of the languages is classed with the other language.
3. A bilingual dictionary with entry words in both languages aimed at speakers of both the languages is classed with the language coming later in 420-490.

Let us try some examples.

German - English Dictionary	**433.21**
Base number	43
Dictionary (Table 4)	-3
Instruction	Add to -3 notation 2-9 from Table 6
English Language (Table 6)	-21
	=43+3+21
Class No.	433.21

(Note: Entry words are in German language)

Rajpal Learners' Hindi-English Dictionary	**491.433 21**
Base number	491.43
Dictionary (Table 4)	-3

Instruction	Add to -3 notation 2-9 from Table 6
English Language (Table 6)	-21
	=491.43+3+21
Class No.	491.433 21

(Note: Entry words are in Hindi language)

Sanskrit- Hindi Dictionary	**491.239 143**
Base number	491.2
Dictionary (Table 4)	-3
Instruction	Add to -3 notation 2-9 from Table 6
Hindi Language (Table 6)	-914 3
	=491.2+3+914 3
Class No.	491.239 143

(Note: Entry words are in Sanskrit language)

German- French Dictionary	**433. 41**
Base number	43
Dictionary (Table 4)	-3
Instruction	Add to -3 notation 2-9 from Table 6
French Language (Table 6)	-41
	=43+3+41
Class No.	433.41

(**Note:** The entry words are in both languages but introduction and explanatory apparatus only in French)

8

Use of Table 5: Ethnic and National Groups

In DDC the Table 5 consists of notations for ethnic and national groups. Like other tables in DDC this table is also never used alone, but may be used as required by add notes or through the interposition of notation 089 from Table 1. There are certain provisions, which require an attention. These are as under:-

1. Except where instructed otherwise, and unless it is redundant, add 0 to the number from this table and to the result add notation 1 or 3-9 from Table 2 for area in which a group is or was located.
2. Standard subdivisions may be added to Table 5 notation when that notation is added directly to the base number. In other words standard subdivisions may be added to the notation from Table 5 when it is added through add note and not through interposition of 089 from Table 1.
3. When notation from Table 5 is not followed by 0 plus notation from Table 2, use 00 for standard subdivision. This is to avoid the confusion whether it is a Table 5

notation or a standard subdivision.

4. Except where instructed otherwise, give preference to the ethnic group over nationality.
5. Except where instructed otherwise, when choosing between two ethnic groups, give preference to the group for which the notation is different from that for the nationality of the people.
6. Except where instructed otherwise, when choosing between two national groups, give preference to the former or ancestral national group.

Examples of use of Table 5 are provided in next few pages.

Ethno psychology of Persians	**155.849 155**
Base number	155.84
Instruction	Add to base number 155.84 notation 1-9 from Table 5
Persians (Table 5)	-915 5
	=155.84+915 5
Class No.	155.849 155

Public opinions of Cypriots	**303.387 895**
Base number	303.387
Instruction	Add to base number 303.387 notation 1-9 from Table 5
Cypriots (Table 5)	-895
	=303.387+895
Class No.	303.387 895

Social status of Brazilians	**305.869 8**
Base number	305.8

Instruction	Add to base number 305.8 notation 1-9 from Table 5
Brazilians (Table 5)	-698
	=305.8+914 2
Class No.	305.869 8
Civil rights of Canadians of British origin	**323.111 12**
Base number	323.11
Instruction	Add to base number 323.11 notation 1-9 from Table 5
Canadians of British origin (Table 5)	-112
	=323.11+112
Class No.	323.111 12
Ethnic cookery of Paharis	**641.592 914 96**
Base number	641.592
Instruction	Add to base number 641.592 notation 1-9 from Table 5
Paharis (Table 5)	-914 96
	=641.592+914 96
Class No.	641.592 914 96
Art of Thai people	**704.039 591 1**
Base number	704.03
Instruction	Add to base number 704.03 notation 1-9 from Table 5
Thai (Table 5)	-959 11

	=704.03+959 1 1
Class No.	704.039 591 1
World history of Filipinos	**909.049 921**
Base number	909.04
Instruction	Add to base number 909.70 notation 1-9 from Table 5
Filipinos (Table 5)	-992 1
	=909.04+992 1
Class No.	909.049 921
Ethno psychology of Sumerians in Canada	**155.849 995 071**
Base number	155.84
Instruction	Add to base number 155.84 notation 1-9 from Table 5
Sumerians (Table 5)	-999 5
Connecting digit	0
Canada (Table 2)	-71
	=155.84+999 5+0+71
Class No.	155.849 995 071
Public opinions of Khmer in China	**303.387 959 320 51**
Base number	303.387
Instruction	Add to base number 303.387 notation 1-9 from Table 5
Khmer (Table 5)	-959 32
Connecting digit	0

China (Table 2)	-51
	=303.387+959 32+0+51
Class No.	303.387 959 320 51
Social status of Ceylonese in Tamil Nadu	**305.891 413 054 82**
Base number	305.8
Instruction	Add to base number 305.8 notation 05-9 from Table 5
Ceylonese (Table 5)	-914 13
Connecting digit	0
Tamil Nadu (Table 2)	-548 2
	=305.8+914 13+0+548 2
Class No.	305.891 413 054 82
Civil rights of Kurds in Afghanistan	**323.119 159 705 81**
Base number	323.11
Instruction	Add to base number 323.11 notation 1-9 from Table 5
Kurds (Table 5)	-915 97
Connecting digit	0
Afghanistan (Table 2)	-581
	=323.11+915 97+0+581
Class No.	323.119 159 705 81
Libraries in the regions where Bhil predominate	**027.017 491 47**
Base number	027.0
Instruction (at .01-.09)	Add to base number

	027.0 the notation 1-9 from Table 2
Regions where specific ethnic (Table 2) and national groups predominate	-174
Instruction	Add to base number -174 notation 1-9 from Table 5
Bhil (Table 5)	-914 7
	=027.0+174+914 7
Class No.	027.017 491 47

Economic history of regions where Kashmiris predominate	**330.917 491 499**
Base number	330.91
Instruction	Add to base number 330.91 the numbers following -1 in notation 11-19 from Table 2
Regions where specific ethnic (Table 2) and national groups predominate	-174
Instruction	Add to base number -174 notation 1-9 from Table 5
Kashmiris (Table 5)	-914 99
	=330.91+74+914 99
Class No.	330.917 491 499

Ethnic cookery of Thai in Zimbabwe	**641.592 959 106 891**
Base number	641.592
Instruction	Add to base number

	641.592 notation 05-9 from Table 5
Thai (Table 5)	-959 1
Connecting digit	0
Zimbabwe (Table 2)	-689 1
	=641.592+959 1+0+689 1
Class No.	641.592 959 106 891
Art of Italians in USA	**704.035 107 3**
Base number	704.03
Instruction	Add to base number 704.03 notation 05-9 from Table 5
Italians (Table 5)	-51
Connecting digit	0
USA (Table 2)	-73
	=704.03+51+0+73
Class No.	704.035 107 3
Romanians folk music	**781.625 91**
Base number	781.62
Instruction	Add to base number 781.62 notation 1-99 from Table 5
Romanians (Table 5)	-591
	=781.62+591
Class No.	781.625 91
Collections of literature by Norwegians	**808.898 398 2**
Base number	808.89

Instruction	Add to base number 808.89 notation -8-9 from Table 3C
Literature for and by persons (Table 3C) of ethnic and national groups	-8
Instruction	Add to -8 notation 1-9 from Table 5
Norwegians (Table 5)	-398 2
	=808.89+8+398 2
Class No.	808.898 398 2
Biographies of Hebrews	**920.009 292 4**
Base number	920.009 2
Instruction	Add to base number 920.009 2 notation 1-9 from Table 5
Hebrews (Table 5)	-924
	=920.009 2+924
Class No.	920.009 292 4
Migration of Panjabis	**304.808 991 421**
Base number	304.8
Standard subdivision	-089
Instruction	Add to base number -089 notation 1-9 from Table 5
Panjabis (Table 5)	-914 21
	=304.8+089+914 21
Class No.	304.808 991 421

Elementary education of Arabs 372.089 927

Base number	372
Standard subdivision	-089
Instruction	Add to base number -089 notation 1-9 from Table 5
Arabs (Table 5)	-927
	=372+089+927
Class No.	372.089 927

Husband-wife relationship of Dutch	**306.872 089 393 1**
Base number	306.872
Standard subdivision	-089
Instruction	Add to base number -089 notation 1-9 from Table 5
Dutch (Table 5)	-393 1
	=306.872+089+393 1
Class No.	306.872 089 393 1

Higher education of Tibetans in Japan	**378.008 995 410 52**
Base number	378
Standard subdivision	-089
Instruction	Add to base number -089 notation 05-9 from Table 5
Tibetans (Table 5)	-954 1
Connecting digit	0
Japan (Table 2)	-52
	=378+008 9+914 95+0+52

Class No.	378.008 995 410 52
Journal of Ethno psychology of Somalis in China	**155.849 354 051 005**
Base number	155.84
Instruction	Add to base number 155.84 notation 1-9 from Table 5
Somalis (Table 5)	-935 4
Connecting digit	0
China (Table 2)	-51
Journal (Table 1)	-005
	=155.84+935 4 + 0 + 51 + 005
Class No.	155.849 354 051 005

(**Note:** At the beginning of Table 2, an instruction is given to use double zeroes for Standard Subdivisions viz: -001-008, hence double zeroes are used for standard subdivisions)

Encyclopaedia of Ethnic cookery of Paharis	**641.592 914 960 03**
Base number	641.592
Instruction	Add to base number 641.592 notation 1-9 from Table 5
Paharis (Table 5)	-914 96
Encyclopaedia (Table 1)	-003
	=641.592+914 96+003
Class No.	641.592 914 960 03

(Note: Because after the notation from table 5 there is no zero and notation from Table 2, hence double zeros are used for standard subdivisions)

Journal on Elementary education of Scandinavians	**372.089 395**
Base number	372
Standard subdivision	-089
Instruction	Add to base number -089 notation 1-9 from Table 5
Scandinavians (Table 5)	-395
	=372+089+395
Class No.	372.089 395

(**Note:** As notation from Table 5 has been added through interposition of -089 from Table 1, hence standard subdivision cannot be added.)

Civil rights of Bengali Indians	**323.119 144**
Base number	323.11
Instruction	Add to base number 323.11 notation 1-9 from Table 5
Bengali (Table 5)	-914 4
	=323.11+914 4
Class No.	323.119 144

(Note: Preference is given to ethnic group.)

Civil rights of Nepalis who become Indian Citizen	**323.119 149 5**
Base number	323.11
Instruction	Add to base number 323.11 notation 1-9 from Table 5
Nepalis (Table 5)	-914 95
	=323.11+914 95
Class No.	323.119 149 5

(Note: Preference is given to ancestral group.)

9

Use of Table 6: Languages

Table 6 in DDC consists of notations for languages. Like other tables in DDC this table is also never used alone, but may be used with those numbers from the schedules and other tables to which the classifier is instructed to add notation from Table 6. Hence notation from Table 6 cannot be added without an instruction. The instructions regarding use of Table 6 are of two types viz. 1. Instructions in the schedules. 2. Instructions in the other tables. You have already used Table 6 while using Table 4. Let us try some more examples.

Libraries in the Burmese speaking regions	**027.017 595 8**
Base number	027.0
Instruction (at .01-.09)	Add to base number 027.0 notation 1-9 from Table 2
Regions where specific (Table 2) languages predominate	-175

Instruction	Add to base number -175 notation 1-9 from Table 6
Burmese language (Table 6)	958
	=027.0+175+958
Class No.	027.017 595 8
Journalism and newspapers in Mongolian speaking regions	**079.175 942 3**
Base number	079
Instruction	Add to base number 079 notation 1-9 from Table 2
Regions where specific (Table 2) languages predominate	-175
Instruction	Add to base number -175 notation 1-9 from Table 6
Mongolian language (Table 6)	942 3
	=079+175+942 3
Class No.	079.175 942 3
Economic history of Korean speaking regions	**330.917 595 7**
Base number	330.91
Instruction	Add to base number 330.91 the numbers following -1 in notation -11-19 from Table 2
Regions where specific (Table 2) languages predominate	-175
Instruction	Add to base number -

	175 notation 1-9 from Table 6
Korean language (Table 6)	957
	=330.91+75+957
Class No.	330.917 595 7
Structural approach to expression of Tamil for Hebrew speaking people	**494.811 824 924**
Base number	494.811
Structural approach to expression for Persons whose native language is different (Table 4)	-824
Instruction	Add to -824 notation 2-9 from Table 6
Hebrew language (Table 6)	-924
	=494.811+824+924
Class No.	494.811 824 924
Audio-lingual approach to expression of Hindi for German speaking people	**491.438 343 1**
Base number	491.43
Audio-lingual approach to expression for Persons whose native language is different (Table 4)	-834
Instruction	Add to -834 notation 2-9 from Table 6
German language (Table 6)	-31
	=491.43+834+31
Class No.	491.438 343 1

Kannada-language primer for peoples whose native language is Swedish	**494.814 864 397**
Base number	494.814
Readers for specific native language speakers (Table 4)	-864
Instruction	Add to -864 notation 2-9 from Table 6
Swedish language (Table 6)	-397
	=494.814+864+397
Class No.	494.814 864 397

Dutch-Danish Dictionary	**439.813 393 1**
Base number	439.81
Dictionary (Table 4)	-3
Instruction	Add to -3 notation 2-9 from Table 6
Dutch Language (Table 6)	-393 1
	=439.81+3+393 1
Class No.	439.813 393 1

Sarita: A Hindi monthly	**059.914 31**
Base number	059
Instruction	Add to base number 059 notation 7-9 from Table 6
Hindi Language (Table 6)	-914 31
	=059+914 31
Class No.	059.914 31

General encyclopaedia in Urdu language	**039.914 39**

Base number	039
Instruction	Add to base number 039 notation 7-9 from Table 6
Urdu Language (Table 6)	-914 39
	=039+914 39
Class No.	039.914 39

Translation of Bible in Bengali	**220.591 44**
Base number	220.5
Instruction (at .53-59)	Add to base number 220.5 notation 3-9 from Table 6
Bengali Language (Table 6)	-914 4
	=220.5+914 4
Class No.	220.591 44

Translation of Bhagavad Gita in Marathi	**294.592 404 591 461**
Base number	294.592 4
Translations	045
Instruction	Add to base number 045 notation 1-9 from Table 6
Marathi Language (Table 6)	-914 61
	=294.592 4+045+914 61
Class No.	294.592 404 591 461

(**Note:** The instructions for classifying translations is provided with the help of * and footnote.)

General bibliographies of Tajik language works	**011.291 57**
Base number	011.2

Instruction	Add to base number 011.2 notation 2-9 from Table 6
Tajik Language (Table 6)	-915 7
	=011.2+915 7
Class No.	011.291 57
Teaching of Russian in Elementary schools	**372.659 171**
Base number	372.65
Instruction (at .552-.659)	Add to base number 372.65 notation 1-9 from Table 6
Russian Language (Table 6)	-917 1
	=372.65+917 1
Class No.	372.659 171
Folk literature in Korean language	**398.204 957**
Base number	398.204
Instruction	Add to base number 398.204 notation 1-9 from Table 6
Korean Language (Table 6)	-957
	=398.204+957
Class No.	398.204 957
Sumerian Proverbs	**398.999 95**
Base number	398.9
Instruction	Add to base number 398.9 notation 1-9 from Table 6
Sumerian Language (Table 6)	-999 5
	=398.9+999 5
Class No.	398.999 95

10

Treatment of Groups of Persons

Table 7 has been deleted from DDC since its 22nd edition. How the numbers, which were previously made by using Table 7 with the help of add instructions, are to be made is dealt in this chapter. The use of Table 7 is replaced by direct use of notation already available in the schedules and in notation 08 from Table 1. The following examples can make it easy to understand how these numbers are to be built?

Programming for mathematicians	**005.102 451**
Base number	005.1
The subject for persons in specific occupations (Table 1)	-024
Instruction	Add to base number -024 notation 001-999
Mathematics	510
	=005.1+024+510
Class No.	005.102 451

Artificial intelligence among Library classificationists	**006.308 802 542**
Base number	006.3
Standard subdivision	-088
Instruction	Add to base number -088 notation 001-999
Library Classification	025.42
	=006.3+088+025.42
Class No.	006.308 802 542
Private libraries in Muslim countries	**027.117 67**
Base number	027.1
Instruction	Add to base number 027.1 notation 1-9 from Table 2
Regions where specific (Table 2) religions predominate	-176
Instruction	Add to base number -176 the numbers following 29 in 292-299
Islam	297
	=027.1+176+7
Class No.	027.117 67
Ethics of biotechnologists	**174.962 082**
Base number	174.9
Instruction	Add to base number 174.9 notation 001-999
Biotechnology	620.82
	=174.9+620.82
Class No.	174.962 082

Opinions of military officers	**303.388 355 331**
Base number	303.388
Instruction	Add to base number 303.388 notation 001-999
Military officers	355.331
	=303.388+355.331
Class No.	303.388 355 331

Women Aeronauts	**305.436 291 3**
Base number	305.43
Instruction	Add to base number 305.43 notation 001-999
Aeronauts	629.13
	=305.43+629.13
Class No.	305.436 291 3

Social status of Panjabi speaking in Canada	**305.791 420 71**
Base number	305.7
Instruction	Add to base number 305.7 notation 1-9 from Table 6; then add 0 and to the result add notation 1-9 from Table 2
Panjabi	914.2
Connecting digit	0
Canada (Table 2)	-71
	=305.6+914.2+0+71
Class No.	305.791 420 71

Social identity of Postal workers	**305.938 34**
Base number	305.9
Instruction	Add to base number 305.9 notation 100-999
Postal organization	383.4
	=305.9+383.4
Class No.	305.938 34
Customs of Airplane flight crews	**390.438 774 044**
Base number	390.4
Instruction	Add to base number 390.4 notation 001-999
Airplane flight crews	387.740 44
	=390.4+387.740 44
Class No.	390.438 774 044
Sacred music of Sikhs	**781.746**
Base number	781.7
Instruction	Add to base number 781.7 the numbers following 29 in 294-299
Sikhism	294.6
	=781.7+46
Class No.	781.746
Composition of preludes for Buddhist services	**782.343 089 281 3**
Base number	782.3
Instruction	Add to base number 782.3 the numbers

	following 29 in 294-299; then add further as follows
Buddhism	~~29~~4.3
Musical form	08
Instruction	Add to 08 the numbers following 784.18 in 784.182-784.189
Preludes†	~~784.189~~ 28
Instruction	Add as instructed under 781.2-781.8
General principles	Add to 1 numbers following 781 in 781.1-781.7
Composition	~~781~~.3
	= 782.3 + 43 + 08 + 928 + 1 + 3
Class No.	782.343 089 281 3
Collections of Slavic novels by Cricketers	**891.830 080 921 796 358**
Base number	891.8
Novels (Table 3B)	-3
Instruction	Add to -300 as instructed under -1-8.
Collections displaying specific features	801-809
Instruction	Add to 80 notation 1-9 from Table 3C
Literature for and by persons of specific (Table 3C) occupations	- 921

Instruction	Add to -921 notation 001-999
Cricket (Schedule)	796.358
	= 891.8 + 300 + 80 + 921 + 796.358
Class No.	891.830 080 921 796 358

Exercise

1. Computer Architecture.
2. World Wide Web
3. Knowledge Engineering
4. Library clerks
5. Keyword indexing
6. Mobile public libraries
7. Musical programs in Museums
8. Self-publishing
9. Mind-body relationship
10. Self-control
11. Professional conduct of judges
12. Hindu-Brahmanical philosophy
13. Plants of nightshade family
14. Zoology of flatfishes
15. Vasectomy for birth control
16. Medical climatology
17. Engineering of artificial satellites
18. Cooking of seafood
19. Live radio programs
20. Drawing comics

21. Virtual Private networks
22. Software packages
23. Interactive video systems
24. Codes for bibliographic description
25. Museum libraries
26. Use of reference books
27. Self-publishing
28. Psychology of Wild children
29. Ethics of judges
30. Early Christian philosophy
31. Radha Soami Satsang
32. Discrimination against women
33. International monetary systems
34. Social service for dependents of military forces personnel
35. Notes for votes
36. Meal service in Inland waterway transportation
37. Map making
38. Triboelectricity
39. Role of water in soil formation
40. Tidal waves
41. Cytology
42. Thermochemistry
43. Astrobiology
44. Plane trees
45. Zoology of Streptoneura
46. Caridea
47. Common herring
48. Weaverbirds
49. Petauridae

50. Gray squirrel
51. Maintence of human body heat
52. Development of vaccines
53. Endocrinology
54. Nature of duties of surgeons
55. Morning after pills for contraception
56. Reflection and refraction of sound
57. Heat exchange engineering
58. Military defense engineering against flooding
59. Aeronautical engineering of drones
60. Use of equipments for fire fighting
61. Tillage after planting
62. Alligator pears crops
63. Horticulture of groundnuts
64. Veterinary science
65. Sewing of sport coats
66. Modern Production Management
67. Management of profit sharing
68. Manufacturing of food cartons
69. Water parks
70. Animal husbandry library
71. Jain temples
72. Library Classification of Management
73. Astrological prediction for personal health of females
74. Aptitude tests for mathematical ability
75. Psychology of visually impaired children
76. Philosophy of Tibetan Buddhism
77. Education in Koran
78. Public opinion of surgeons

79. Women astronauts
80. Industrial relations in hotels
81. Conservation and Protection of sea tongue less frogs
82. Training of civilian staff in military
83. Investigation in rape case
84. Academic status of secondary school teachers
85. Domestic trade of flowers
86. Customs for Sikh holidays
87. Handbook of Mechanical Engineering
88. Magnetic properties of plasmas
89. Thermal properties of electrolytic solutions
90. Mesozoic era paleobotany
91. Organisms characteristic of meadows
92. Reproductive adaptation in roses
93. Population biology of Termites
94. Drugs derived from Aloe Vera
95. Treatment of cholera by diathermy
96. Surgical complications of kidney surgery
97. Optical diagnosis of breast cancer
98. Roman architecture for temporary buildings
99. Interior lighting for hotel buildings
100. Irrigation of soybeans
101. Construction night suits for children
102. Umpiring in Volleyball
103. Public relations in universities
104. Pigeon hunting as a game
105. Treaties between China and Pakistan
106. Court decisions on abortion in USA
107. Administrative regulations for environmental protection in Turkey

108. Fees for legal professional services in high courts of Japan
109. World history of Gonds in 15th century
110. Geography of Tamil Nadu
111. Biography of Paharis
112. History of India during Akbar
113. History of Andhra Pradesh during 20th century
114. History of Pakistan under Musharaf
115. Science journals
116. Encyclopedia of Photography
117. Research on Library classification
118. Terminology used in labour economics
119. Libraries in 14th century
120. Outline of DDC
121. Use of cartoons in journalism
122. Mathematics for Engineers
123. Statistical methods for Chemical engineering
124. Exhibition of underwater photographs
125. University libraries in Gujarat
126. Migration of people from China to Canada
127. Political conditions in Pakistan
128. Military assistance to New Zealand
129. Flora of Angola
130. Conservation of land in Libya
131. Social problems in Sri Lanka
132. Geodetic surveying in Bhutan
133. Special libraries in Albania
134. Librarianship as a profession in Colombia
135. Russian poetry in 20th century
136. Collection of Bengali detective fictions

137. Spellings and pronunciation of Norwegian language
138. Panjabi words in Tamil language
139. Translating from German to English language
140. Audio-lingual approach to expression of Czech language for Pahari speaking people
141. French-language reader on colour photography for those whose native language is not French
142. Marathi-language primer on Classification for those whose native language is Nepali
143. Hindi-Russian dictionary
144. Social stratification of Panjabis
145. Ethnic cookery of Italians in China
146. Collection of literature by Persians
147. Ethics of Library classifiers
148. Public opinion of the Supreme Court judges
149. Sacred music of Sufism
150. Collection of English fictions by Footballers

ANSWERS TO EXERCISE

1.	004.35	2.	004.678
3.	006.332	4.	023.3
5.	025.486	6.	027.42
7.	069.16	8.	070.593
9.	124.2	10.	153.8
11.	174.3	12.	181.4
13.	583.952	14.	597.69
15.	613.942	16.	616.988
17.	629.46	18.	641.692
19.	791.443	20.	741.5
21.	007.678	22.	005.3
23.	006.7	24.	025.324
25.	027.68	26.	028.7
27.	070.593	28.	155.456 7
29.	174.3	30.	189
31.	294	32.	305.42
33.	332.45	34.	355.34
35.	364.132 4	36.	386.242
37.	526	38.	537.21
39.	551.305	40.	551.463 7
41.	571.6	42.	572.436
43.	576.839	44.	583.44
45.	594.32	46.	595.388
47.	597.452	48.	598.887
49.	599.23	50.	599.362
51.	612.014 26	52.	615.372
53.	616.4	54.	617.023 2
55.	618.182 5	56.	620.21

57. 621.402 2
58. 623.31
59. 623.746 9
60. 628.925
61. 631.51
62. 634.653
63. 635.659 6
64. 636.089
65. 646.433
66. 658.5
67. 658.322 5
68. 676.34
69. 797.2
70. 026.636
71. 294.435
72. 025.466 58
73. 133.586 130 424
74. 153.945 1
75. 155.451 1
76. 181.043 923
77. 297.122 837
78. 303.388 617
79. 305.436 294 5
80. 331.041 647 94
81. 333.957 865 16
82. 355.619 69
83. 363.259 532
84. 373.110 4
85. 381.456 359
86. 394.265 46
87. 621
88. 530.442
89. 541.374 6
90. 561.116
91. 578.746
92. 583.734 146
93. 595.736 178 8
94. 615.324 352
95. 616.932 063 23
96. 617.461 042 1
97. 616.994 490 754 5
98. 722.704 44
99. 621.322 85
100. 633.348 7
101. 646.475 06
102. 796.325 3
103. 659.293 78
104. 799.248 65
105. 341.026 651 054 91
106. 342.730 840 264 3
107. 344.561 063 670 263 6
108. 347.520 335 72
109. 909.049 482 34
110. 915.482
111. 920.091 496
112. 954.025 4
113. 954.840 4
114. 954.910 53

115. 505
116. 770.3
117. 025.430 72
118. 331.014
119. 027.009 023
120. 028.431 021 8
121. 070.402 22
122. 510.246 2
123. 660.072 7
124. 778.730 74
125. 027.754 75
126. 304.751 071
127. 320.954 91
128. 355.032 93
129. 581.967 3
130. 333.720 961 2
131. 361.109 549 3
132. 526.309 549 8
133. 026.000 949 65
134. 020.238 61
135. 891.714
136. 891.443 087 208
137. 439.828 13
138. 494.811 249 142
139. 428.023 1
140. 491.868 349 149 6
141. 448.640 247 786
142. 491.461 864 914 95 024 025 43
143. 491.433 917 1
144. 305.891 421
145. 641.592 510 51
146. 808.898 915 5
147. 174.702 543
148. 303.388 347 035 34
149. 781.729 74
150. 823.008 092 179 633

Summaries

FIRST SUMMARY
The Ten Main Classes

000 Computer science, information & general works
100 Philosophy & psychology
200 Religion
300 Social sciences
400 Language
500 Science
600 Technology
700 Arts & recreation
800 Literature
900 History & geography

SECOND SUMMARY

The Hundred Divisions

000 Computer science, knowledge & systems
010 Bibliographies
020 Library & information sciences
030 Encyclopedias & books of facts
040 [Unassigned]
050 Magazines, journals & serials
060 Associations, organizations & museums
070 News media, journalism & publishing
080 Quotations
090 Manuscripts & rare books

100 Philosophy
110 Metaphysics
120 Epistemology
130 Parapsychology & occultism
140 Philosophical schools of thought
150 Psychology
160 Logic
170 Ethics
180 Ancient, medieval & eastern philosophy
190 Modern western philosophy

200 Religion
210 Philosophy & theory of religion
220 The Bible
230 Christianity & Christian theology
240 Christian practice & observance
250 Christian pastoral practice & religious orders

260 Christian organization, social work & worship
270 History of Christianity
280 Christian denominations
290 Other religions

300 Social sciences, sociology & anthropology
310 Statistics
320 Political science
330 Economics
340 Law
350 Public administration & military science
360 Social problems & social services
370 Education
380 Commerce, communications & transportation
390 Customs, etiquette & folklore

400 Language
410 Linguistics
420 English & Old English languages
430 German & related languages
440 French & related languages
450 Italian, Romanian & related languages
460 Spanish & Portuguese languages
470 Latin & Italic languages
480 Classical & modern Greek languages
490 Other languages

500 Science
510 Mathematics
520 Astronomy
530 Physics
540 Chemistry
550 Earth sciences & geology
560 Fossils & prehistoric life
570 Life sciences; biology
580 Plants (Botany)
590 Animals (Zoology)

600 Technology
610 Medicine & health
620 Engineering
630 Agriculture
640 Home & family management
650 Management & public relations
660 Chemical engineering
670 Manufacturing
680 Manufacture for specific uses
690 Building & construction

700 Arts
710 Landscaping & area planning
720 Architecture
730 Sculpture, ceramics & metalwork
740 Drawing & decorative arts
750 Painting
760 Graphic arts
770 Photography & computer art

780 Music
790 Sports, games & entertainment

800 Literature, rhetoric & criticism
810 American literature in English
820 English & Old English literatures
830 German & related literatures
840 French & related literatures
850 Italian, Romanian & related literatures
860 Spanish & Portuguese literatures
870 Latin & Italic literatures
880 Classical & modern Greek literatures
890 Other literatures

900 History
910 Geography & travel
920 Biography & genealogy
930 History of ancient world (to ca. 499)
940 History of Europe
950 History of Asia
960 History of Africa
970 History of North America
980 History of South America
990 History of other areas

THIRD SUMMARY

The Thousand Sections

000 Computer science, information & general works

001 Knowledge

002 The book

003 Systems

004 Data processing & computer science

005 Computer programming, programs & data

006 Special computer methods

007 [Unassigned]

008 [Unassigned]

009 [Unassigned]

010 Bibliography

011 Bibliographies

012 Bibliographies of individuals

013 [Unassigned]

014 Of anonymous & pseudonymous works

015 Bibliographies of works from specific places

016 Bibliographies of works on specific subjects

017 General subject catalogs

018 Catalogs arranged by author, date, etc.

019 Dictionary catalogs

020 Library & information sciences

021 Library relationships

022 Administration of physical plant

023 Personnel management

024 [Unassigned]

025 Library operations

026 Libraries for specific subjects
027 General libraries
028 Reading & use of other information media
029 [Unassigned]

030 General encyclopedic works
031 Encyclopedias in American English
032 Encyclopedias in English
033 In other Germanic languages
034 Encyclopedias in French, Occitan & Catalan
035 In Italian, Romanian & related languages
036 Encyclopedias in Spanish & Portuguese
037 Encyclopedias in Slavic languages
038 Encyclopedias in Scandinavian languages
039 Encyclopedias in other languages

040 [Unassigned]
041 [Unassigned]
042 [Unassigned]
043 [Unassigned]
044 [Unassigned]
045 [Unassigned]
046 [Unassigned]
047 [Unassigned]
048 [Unassigned]
049 [Unassigned]

050 General serial publications
051 Serials in American English
052 Serials in English

053 Serials in other Germanic languages
054 Serials in French, Occitan & Catalan
055 In Italian, Romanian & related languages
056 Serials in Spanish & Portuguese
057 Serials in Slavic languages
058 Serials in Scandinavian languages
059 Serials in other languages

060 General organizations & museum science
061 Organizations in North America
062 Organizations in British Isles; in England
063 Organizations in central Europe; in Germany
064 Organizations in France & Monaco
065 Organizations in Italy & adjacent islands
066 In Iberian Peninsula & adjacent islands
067 Organizations in eastern Europe; in Russia
068 Organizations in other geographic areas
069 Museum science

070 News media, journalism & publishing
071 Newspapers in North America
072 Newspapers in British Isles; in England
073 Newspapers in central Europe; in Germany
074 Newspapers in France & Monaco
075 Newspapers in Italy & adjacent islands
076 In Iberian Peninsula & adjacent islands
077 Newspapers in eastern Europe; in Russia
078 Newspapers in Scandinavia
079 Newspapers in other geographic areas

080 General collections

081 Collections in American English

082 Collections in English

083 Collections in other Germanic languages

084 Collections in French, Occitan & Catalan

085 In Italian, Romanian & related languages

086 Collections in Spanish & Portuguese

087 Collections in Slavic languages

088 Collections in Scandinavian languages

089 Collections in other languages

090 Manuscripts & rare books

091 Manuscripts

092 Block books

093 Incunabula

094 Printed books

095 Books notable for bindings

096 Books notable for illustrations

097 Books notable for ownership or origin

098 Prohibited works, forgeries & hoaxes

099 Books notable for format

PHILOSOPHY AND PSYCHOLOGY

100 Philosophy & psychology

101 Theory of philosophy

102 Miscellany

103 Dictionaries & encyclopedias

104 [Unassigned]

105 Serial publications

106 Organizations & management

107 Education, research & related topics

108 Kinds of persons treatment

109 Historical & collected persons treatment

110 Metaphysics

111 Ontology

112 [Unassigned]

113 Cosmology

114 Space

115 Time

116 Change

117 Structure

118 Force & energy

119 Number & quantity

120 Epistemology, causation & humankind

121 Epistemology

122 Causation

123 Determinism & indeterminism

124 Teleology

125 [Unassigned]

126 The self

127 The unconscious & the subconscious

128 Humankind

129 Origin & destiny of individual souls

130 Parapsychology & occultism

131 Parapsychological & occult methods

132 [Unassigned]

133 Specific topics in parapsychology & occultism

134 [Unassigned]

135 Dreams & mysteries

136 [Unassigned]

137 Divinatory graphology

138 Physiognomy

139 Phrenology

140 Specific philosophical schools

141 Idealism & related systems

142 Critical philosophy

143 Bergsonism & intuitionism

144 Humanism & related systems

145 Sensationalism

146 Naturalism & related systems

147 Pantheism & related systems

148 Eclecticism, liberalism & traditionalism

149 Other philosophical systems

150 Psychology

151 [Unassigned]

152 Perception, movement, emotions & drives

153 Mental processes & intelligence
154 Subconscious & altered states
155 Differential & developmental psychology
156 Comparative psychology
157 [Unassigned]
158 Applied psychology
159 [Unassigned]

160 Logic

161 Induction
162 Deduction
163 [Unassigned]
164 [Unassigned]
165 Fallacies & sources of error
166 Syllogisms
167 Hypotheses
168 Argument & persuasion
169 Analogy

170 Ethics

171 Ethical systems
172 Political ethics
173 Ethics of family relationships
174 Occupational ethics
175 Ethics of recreation & leisure
176 Ethics of sex & reproduction
177 Ethics of social relations
178 Ethics of consumption
179 Other ethical norms

180 Ancient, medieval & eastern philosophy

181 Eastern philosophy

182 Pre-Socratic Greek philosophies

183 Socratic & related philosophies

184 Platonic philosophy

185 Aristotelian philosophy

186 Skeptic & Neoplatonic philosophies

187 Epicurean philosophy

188 Stoic philosophy

189 Medieval western philosophy

190 Modern western philosophy

191 Philosophy of United States & Canada

192 Philosophy of British Isles

193 Philosophy of Germany & Austria

194 Philosophy of France

195 Philosophy of Italy

196 Philosophy of Spain & Portugal

197 Philosophy of former Soviet Union

198 Philosophy of Scandinavia

199 Philosophy in other geographic areas

RELIGION

200 Religion

201 Religious mythology & social theology

202 Doctrines

203 Public worship & other practices

204 Religious experience, life & practice

205 Religious ethics

206 Leaders & organization

207 Missions & religious education

208 Sources

209 Sects & reform movements

210 Philosophy & theory of religion

211 Concepts of God

212 Existence, knowability & attributes of God

213 Creation

214 Theodicy

215 Science & religion

216 [Unassigned]

217 [Unassigned]

218 Humankind

219 [Unassigned]

220 Bible

221 Old Testament (Tanakh)

222 Historical books of Old Testament

223 Poetic books of Old Testament

224 Prophetic books of Old Testament

225 New Testament

226 Gospels & Acts

227 Epistles

228 Revelation (Apocalypse)

229 Apocrypha & pseudepigrapha

230 Christianity & Christian theology

231 God

232 Jesus Christ & his family

233 Humankind

234 Salvation & grace

235 Spiritual beings

236 Eschatology

237 [Unassigned]

238 Creeds & catechisms

239 Apologetics & polemics

240 Christian moral & devotional theology

241 Christian ethics

242 Devotional literature

243 Evangelistic writings for individuals

244 [Unassigned]

245 [Unassigned]

246 Use of art in Christianity

247 Church furnishings & articles

248 Christian experience, practice & life

249 Christian observances in family life

250 Christian orders & local church

251 Preaching

252 Texts of sermons

253 Pastoral office & work
254 Parish administration
255 Religious congregations & orders
256 [Unassigned]
257 [Unassigned]
258 [Unassigned]
259 Pastoral care of families & kinds of persons

260 Social & ecclesiastical theology

261 Social theology
262 Ecclesiology
263 Days, times & places of observance
264 Public worship
265 Sacraments, other rites & acts
266 Missions
267 Associations for religious work
268 Religious education
269 Spiritual renewal

270 History of Christianity & Christian church

271 Religious orders in church history
272 Persecutions in church history
273 Doctrinal controversies & heresies
274 History of Christianity in Europe
275 History of Christianity in Asia
276 History of Christianity in Africa
277 History of Christianity in North America
278 History of Christianity in South America
279 History of Christianity in other areas

280 Christian denominations & sects

281 Early church & Eastern churches

282 Roman Catholic Church

283 Anglican churches

284 Protestants of Continental origin

285 Presbyterian, Reformed & Congregational

286 Baptist, Disciples of Christ & Adventist

287 Methodist & related churches

288 [Unassigned]

289 Other denominations & sects

290 Other religions

291 [Unassigned]

292 Greek & Roman religion

293 Germanic religion

294 Religions of Indic origin

295 Zoroastrianism

296 Judaism

297 Islam, Babism & Bahai Faith

298 (Optional number)

299 Religions not provided for elsewhere

SOCIAL SCIENCES

300 Social sciences
301 Sociology & anthropology
302 Social interaction
303 Social processes
304 Factors affecting social behavior
305 Social groups
306 Culture & institutions
307 Communities
308 [Unassigned]
309 [Unassigned]

310 Collections of general statistics
311 [Unassigned]
312 [Unassigned]
313 [Unassigned]
314 General statistics of Europe
315 General statistics of Asia
316 General statistics of Africa
317 General statistics of North America
318 General statistics of South America
319 General statistics of other areas

320 Political science
321 Systems of governments & states
322 Relation of state to organized groups
323 Civil & political rights
324 The political process

325 International migration & colonization
326 Slavery & emancipation
327 International relations
328 The legislative process
329 [Unassigned]

330 Economics
331 Labor economics
332 Financial economics
333 Economics of land & energy
334 Cooperatives
335 Socialism & related systems
336 Public finance
337 International economics
338 Production
339 Macroeconomics & related topics

340 Law
341 Law of nations
342 Constitutional & administrative law
343 Military, tax, trade & industrial law
344 Labor, social, education & cultural law
345 Criminal law
346 Private law
347 Civil procedure & courts
348 Laws, regulations & cases
349 Law of specific jurisdictions & areas

350 Public administration & military science
351 Public administration

352 General considerations of public administration
353 Specific fields of public administration
354 Administration of economy & environment
355 Military science
356 Infantry forces & warfare
357 Mounted forces & warfare
358 Air & other specialized forces
359 Sea forces & warfare

360 Social problems & services; associations
361 Social problems & social welfare in general
362 Social welfare problems & services
363 Other social problems & services
364 Criminology
365 Penal & related institutions
366 Associations
367 General clubs
368 Insurance
369 Miscellaneous kinds of associations

370 Education
371 Schools & their activities; special education
372 Elementary education
373 Secondary education
374 Adult education
375 Curricula
376 [Unassigned]
377 [Unassigned]
378 Higher education
379 Public policy issues in education

380 Commerce, communications & transportation

381 Commerce

382 International commerce

383 Postal communication

384 Communications; telecommunication

385 Railroad transportation

386 Inland waterway & ferry transportation

387 Water, air & space transportation

388 Transportation; ground transportation

389 Metrology & standardization

390 Customs, etiquette & folklore

391 Costume & personal appearance

392 Customs of life cycle & domestic life

393 Death customs

394 General customs

395 Etiquette (Manners)

396 [Unassigned]

397 [Unassigned]

398 Folklore

399 Customs of war & diplomacy

LANGUAGE

400 Language

401 Philosophy & theory

402 Miscellany

403 Dictionaries & encyclopedias

404 Special topics

405 Serial publications

406 Organizations & management

407 Education, research & related topics

408 Kinds of persons treatment

409 Geographic & persons treatment

410 Linguistics

411 Writing systems

412 Etymology

413 Dictionaries

414 Phonology & phonetics

415 Grammar

416 [Unassigned]

417 Dialectology & historical linguistics

418 Standard usage & applied linguistics

419 Sign languages

420 English & Old English

421 English writing system & phonology

422 English etymology

423 English dictionaries

424 [Unassigned]

425 English grammar

426 [Unassigned]
427 English language variations
428 Standard English usage
429 Old English (Anglo-Saxon)

430 Germanic languages; German
431 German writing systems & phonology
432 German etymology
433 German dictionaries
434 [Unassigned]
435 German grammar
436 [Unassigned]
437 German language variations
438 Standard German usage
439 Other Germanic languages

440 Romance languages; French
441 French writing systems & phonology
442 French etymology
443 French dictionaries
444 [Unassigned]
445 French grammar
446 [Unassigned]
447 French language variations
448 Standard French usage
449 Occitan & Catalan

450 Italian, Romanian & related languages
451 Italian writing systems & phonology
452 Italian etymology

453 Italian dictionaries
454 [Unassigned]
455 Italian grammar
456 [Unassigned]
457 Italian language variations
458 Standard Italian usage
459 Romanian & related languages

460 Spanish & Portuguese languages
461 Spanish writing systems & phonology
462 Spanish etymology
463 Spanish dictionaries
464 [Unassigned]
465 Spanish grammar
466 [Unassigned]
467 Spanish language variations
468 Standard Spanish usage
469 Portuguese

470 Italic languages; Latin
471 Classical Latin writing & phonology
472 Classical Latin etymology
473 Classical Latin dictionaries
474 [Unassigned]
475 Classical Latin grammar
476 [Unassigned]
477 Old, postclassical & Vulgar Latin
478 Classical Latin usage
479 Other Italic languages

480 Hellenic languages; classical Greek

481 Classical Greek writing & phonology

482 Classical Greek etymology

483 Classical Greek dictionaries

484 [Unassigned]

485 Classical Greek grammar

486 [Unassigned]

487 Preclassical & postclassical Greek

488 Classical Greek usage

489 Other Hellenic languages

490 Other languages

491 East Indo-European & Celtic languages

492 Afro-Asiatic languages; Semitic languages

493 Non-Semitic Afro-Asiatic languages

494 Altaic, Uralic, Hyperborean & Dravidian

495 Languages of East & Southeast Asia

496 African languages

497 North American native languages

498 South American native languages

499 Austronesian & other languages

NATURAL SCIENCES & MATHEMATICS

500 Natural sciences & mathematics
501 Philosophy & theory
502 Miscellany
503 Dictionaries & encyclopedias
504 [Unassigned]
505 Serial publications
506 Organizations & management
507 Education, research & related topics
508 Natural history
509 Historical, geographic & persons treatment

510 Mathematics
511 General principles of mathematics
512 Algebra
513 Arithmetic
514 Topology
515 Analysis
516 Geometry
517 [Unassigned]
518 Numerical analysis
519 Probabilities & applied mathematics

520 Astronomy & allied sciences
521 Celestial mechanics
522 Techniques, equipment & materials
523 Specific celestial bodies & phenomena
524 [Unassigned]
525 Earth (Astronomical geography)

526 Mathematical geography
527 Celestial navigation
528 Ephemerides
529 Chronology

530 Physics
531 Classical mechanics; solid mechanics
532 Fluid mechanics; liquid mechanics
533 Gas mechanics
534 Sound & related vibrations
535 Light & infrared & ultraviolet phenomena
536 Heat
537 Electricity & electronics
538 Magnetism
539 Modern physics

540 Chemistry & allied sciences
541 Physical chemistry
542 Techniques, equipment & materials
543 Analytical chemistry
544 [Unassigned]
545 [Unassigned]
546 Inorganic chemistry
547 Organic chemistry
548 Crystallography
549 Mineralogy

550 Earth sciences
551 Geology, hydrology & meteorology
552 Petrology
553 Economic geology

554 Earth sciences of Europe
555 Earth sciences of Asia
556 Earth sciences of Africa
557 Earth sciences of North America
558 Earth sciences of South America
559 Earth sciences of other areas

560 Paleontology; paleozoology
561 Paleobotany; fossil microorganisms
562 Fossil invertebrates
563 Fossil marine & seashore invertebrates
564 Fossil mollusks & molluscoids
565 Fossil arthropods
566 Fossil chordates
567 Fossil cold-blooded vertebrates; fossil fishes
568 Fossil birds
569 Fossil mammals

570 Life sciences; biology
571 Physiology & related subjects
572 Biochemistry
573 Specific physiological systems in animals
574 [Unassigned]
575 Specific parts of & systems in plants
576 Genetics & evolution
577 Ecology
578 Natural history of organisms
579 Microorganisms, fungi & algae

580 Plants (Botany)

581 Specific topics in natural history
582 Plants noted for characteristics & flowers
583 Dicotyledons
584 Monocotyledons
585 Gymnosperms; conifers
586 Seedless plants
587 Vascular seedless plants
588 Bryophytes
589 [Unassigned]

590 Animals (Zoology)
591 Specific topics in natural history
592 Invertebrates
593 Marine & seashore invertebrates
594 Mollusks & molluscoids
595 Arthropods
596 Chordates
597 Cold-blooded vertebrates; fishes
598 Birds
599 Mammals

TECHNOLOGY

600 Technology

601 Philosophy & theory

602 Miscellany

603 Dictionaries & encyclopedias

604 Special topics

605 Serial publications

606 Organizations

607 Education, research & related topics

608 Inventions & patents

609 Historical, geographic & persons treatment

610 Medicine & health

611 Human anatomy, cytology & histology

612 Human physiology

613 Personal health & safety

614 Incidence & prevention of disease

615 Pharmacology & therapeutics

616 Diseases

617 Surgery & related medical specialties

618 Gynecology, obstetrics, pediatrics & geriatrics

619 [Unassigned]

620 Engineering & allied operations

621 Applied physics

622 Mining & related operations

623 Military & nautical engineering

624 Civil engineering

625 Engineering of railroads & roads
626 [Unassigned]
627 Hydraulic engineering
628 Sanitary & municipal engineering
629 Other branches of engineering

630 Agriculture & related technologies
631 Techniques, equipment & materials
632 Plant injuries, diseases & pests
633 Field & plantation crops
634 Orchards, fruits & forestry
635 Garden crops (Horticulture)
636 Animal husbandry
637 Processing dairy & related products
638 Insect culture
639 Hunting, fishing & conservation

640 Home & family management
641 Food & drink
642 Meals & table service
643 Housing & household equipment
644 Household utilities
645 Household furnishings
646 Sewing, clothing & personal living
647 Management of public households
648 Housekeeping
649 Child rearing & home care of persons

650 Management & auxiliary services
651 Office services

652 Processes of written communication

653 Shorthand

654 [Unassigned]

655 [Unassigned]

656 [Unassigned]

657 Accounting

658 General management

659 Advertising & public relations

660 Chemical engineering

661 Industrial chemicals

662 Explosives, fuels & related products

663 Beverage technology

664 Food technology

665 Industrial oils, fats, waxes & gases

666 Ceramic & allied technologies

667 Cleaning, color & coating technologies

668 Technology of other organic products

669 Metallurgy

670 Manufacturing

671 Metalworking & primary metal products

672 Iron, steel & other iron alloys

673 Nonferrous metals

674 Lumber processing, wood products & cork

675 Leather & fur processing

676 Pulp & paper technology

677 Textiles

678 Elastomers & elastomer products

679 Other products of specific materials

680 Manufacture for specific uses

681 Precision instruments & other devices

682 Small forge work (Blacksmithing)

683 Hardware & household appliances

684 Furnishings & home workshops

685 Leather, fur goods & related products

686 Printing & related activities

687 Clothing & accessories

688 Other final products & packaging

689 [Unassigned]

690 Buildings

691 Building materials

692 Auxiliary construction practices

693 Specific materials & purposes

694 Wood construction & carpentry

695 Roof covering

696 Utilities

697 Heating, ventilating & air-conditioning

698 Detail finishing

699 [Unassigned]

ARTS & RECREATION

700 The arts; fine & decorative arts

701 Philosophy of fine & decorative arts

702 Miscellany of fine & decorative arts

703 Dictionaries of fine & decorative arts

704 Special topics in fine & decorative arts

705 Serial publications of fine & decorative arts

706 Organizations & management

707 Education, research & related topics

708 Galleries, museums & private collections

709 Historical, geographic & persons treatment

710 Civic & landscape art

711 Area planning

712 Landscape architecture

713 Landscape architecture of trafficways

714 Water features

715 Woody plants

716 Herbaceous plants

717 Structures in landscape architecture

718 Landscape design of cemeteries

719 Natural landscapes

720 Architecture

721 Architectural structure

722 Architecture to ca. 300

723 Architecture from ca. 300 to 1399

724 Architecture from 1400

725 Public structures
726 Buildings for religious purposes
727 Buildings for education & research
728 Residential & related buildings
729 Design & decoration

730 Plastic arts; sculpture
731 Processes, forms & subjects of sculpture
732 Sculpture to ca. 500
733 Greek, Etruscan & Roman sculpture
734 Sculpture from ca. 500 to 1399
735 Sculpture from 1400
736 Carving & carvings
737 Numismatics & sigillography
738 Ceramic arts
739 Art metalwork

740 Drawing & decorative arts
741 Drawing & drawings
742 Perspective
743 Drawing & drawings by subject
744 [Unassigned]
745 Decorative arts
746 Textile arts
747 Interior decoration
748 Glass
749 Furniture & accessories

750 Painting & paintings
751 Techniques, equipment, materials & forms

752 Color

753 Symbolism, allegory, mythology & legend

754 Genre paintings

755 Religion

756 [Unassigned]

757 Human figures

758 Other subjects

759 Historical, geographic & persons treatment

760 Graphic arts; printmaking & prints

761 Relief processes (Block printing)

762 [Unassigned]

763 Lithographic processes

764 Chromolithography & serigraphy

765 Metal engraving

766 Mezzotinting, aquatinting & related processes

767 Etching & drypoint

768 [Unassigned]

769 Prints

770 Photography, photographs & computer art

771 Techniques, equipment & materials

772 Metallic salt processes

773 Pigment processes of printing

774 Holography

775 Digital photography

776 Computer art (Digital art)

777 [Unassigned]

778 Fields & kinds of photography

779 Photographs

780 Music

781 General principles & musical forms

782 Vocal music

783 Music for single voices; the voice

784 Instruments & instrumental ensembles

785 Ensembles with one instrument per part

786 Keyboard & other instruments

787 Stringed instruments

788 Wind instruments

789 (Optional number)

790 Recreational & performing arts

791 Public performances

792 Stage presentations

793 Indoor games & amusements

794 Indoor games of skill

795 Games of chance

796 Athletic & outdoor sports & games

797 Aquatic & air sports

798 Equestrian sports & animal racing

799 Fishing, hunting & shooting

LITERATURE

800 Literature & rhetoric

801 Philosophy & theory

802 Miscellany

803 Dictionaries & encyclopedias

804 [Unassigned]

805 Serial publications

806 Organizations & management

807 Education, research & related topics

808 Rhetoric & collections of literature

809 History, description & criticism

810 American literature in English

811 American poetry in English

812 American drama in English

813 American fiction in English

814 American essays in English

815 American speeches in English

816 American letters in English

817 American humor & satire in English

818 American miscellaneous writings

819 (Optional number)

820 English & Old English literatures

821 English poetry

822 English drama

823 English fiction

824 English essays

825 English speeches
826 English letters
827 English humor & satire
828 English miscellaneous writings
829 Old English (Anglo-Saxon)

830 Literatures of Germanic languages
831 German poetry
832 German drama
833 German fiction
834 German essays
835 German speeches
836 German letters
837 German humor & satire
838 German miscellaneous writings
839 Other Germanic literatures

840 Literatures of Romance languages
841 French poetry
842 French drama
843 French fiction
844 French essays
845 French speeches
846 French letters
847 French humor & satire
848 French miscellaneous writings
849 Occitan & Catalan literatures

850 Italian, Romanian & related literatures
851 Italian poetry

852 Italian drama
853 Italian fiction
854 Italian essays
855 Italian speeches
856 Italian letters
857 Italian humor & satire
858 Italian miscellaneous writings
859 Romanian & related literatures

860 Spanish & Portuguese literatures
861 Spanish poetry
862 Spanish drama
863 Spanish fiction
864 Spanish essays
865 Spanish speeches
866 Spanish letters
867 Spanish humor & satire
868 Spanish miscellaneous writings
869 Portuguese literature

870 Italic literatures; Latin literature
871 Latin poetry
872 Latin dramatic poetry & drama
873 Latin epic poetry & fiction
874 Latin lyric poetry
875 Latin speeches
876 Latin letters
877 Latin humor & satire
878 Latin miscellaneous writings
879 Literatures of other Italic languages

880 Hellenic literatures; classical Greek

881 Classical Greek poetry

882 Classical Greek dramatic poetry & drama

883 Classical Greek epic poetry & fiction

884 Classical Greek lyric poetry

885 Classical Greek speeches

886 Classical Greek letters

887 Classical Greek humor & satire

888 Classical Greek miscellaneous writings

889 Modern Greek literature

890 Literatures of other languages

891 East Indo-European & Celtic literatures

892 Afro-Asiatic literatures; Semitic literatures

893 Non-Semitic Afro-Asiatic literatures

894 Altaic, Uralic, Hyperborean & Dravidian

895 Literatures of East & Southeast Asia

896 African literatures

897 North American native literatures

898 South American native literatures

899 Austronesian & other literatures

HISTORY AND GEOGRAPHY

900 History & geography

901 Philosophy & theory

902 Miscellany

903 Dictionaries & encyclopedias

904 Collected accounts of events

905 Serial publications

906 Organizations & management

907 Education, research & related topics

908 Kinds of persons treatment

909 World history

910 Geography & travel

911 Historical geography

912 Atlases, maps, charts & plans

913 Geography of & travel in ancient world

914 Geography of & travel in Europe

915 Geography of & travel in Asia

916 Geography of & travel in Africa

917 Geography of & travel in North America

918 Geography of & travel in South America

919 Geography of & travel in other areas

920 Biography, genealogy & insignia

921 (Optional number)

922 (Optional number)

923 (Optional number)

924 (Optional number)

925 (Optional number)

926 (Optional number)

927 (Optional number)

928 (Optional number)

929 Genealogy, names & insignia

930 History of ancient world to ca. 499

931 China to 420

932 Egypt to 640

933 Palestine to 70

934 India to 647

935 Mesopotamia & Iranian Plateau to 637

936 Europe north & west of Italy to ca. 499

937 Italy & adjacent territories to 476

938 Greece to 323

939 Other parts of ancient world to ca. 640

940 History of Europe

941 British Isles

942 England & Wales

943 Central Europe; Germany

944 France & Monaco

945 Italian Peninsula & adjacent islands

946 Iberian Peninsula & adjacent islands

947 Eastern Europe; Russia

948 Scandinavia

949 Other parts of Europe

950 History of Asia; Far East

951 China & adjacent areas

952 Japan

953 Arabian Peninsula & adjacent areas

954 South Asia; India

955 Iran

956 Middle East (Near East)

957 Siberia (Asiatic Russia)

958 Central Asia

959 Southeast Asia

960 History of Africa

961 Tunisia & Libya

962 Egypt & Sudan

963 Ethiopia & Eritrea

964 Northwest African coast & offshore islands

965 Algeria

966 West Africa & offshore islands

967 Central Africa & offshore islands

968 Southern Africa; Republic of South Africa

969 South Indian Ocean islands

970 History of North America

971 Canada

972 Middle America; Mexico

973 United States

974 Northeastern United States

975 Southeastern United States

976 South central United States

977 North central United States

978 Western United States

979 Great Basin & Pacific Slope region

980 History of South America

981 Brazil

982 Argentina

983 Chile

984 Bolivia

985 Peru

986 Colombia & Ecuador

987 Venezuela

988 Guiana

989 Paraguay & Uruguay

990 History of other areas

991 [Unassigned]

992 [Unassigned]

993 New Zealand

994 Australia

995 Melanesia; New Guinea

996 Other parts of Pacific; Polynesia

997 Atlantic Ocean islands

998 Arctic islands & Antarctica

999 Extraterrestrial worlds